D0239757

THE ROBBER
OF MEMORIES

Also by Michael Jacobs from Granta Books

Andes

THE ROBBER
OF MEMORIES

A River Journey through Colombia

MICHAEL JACOBS

GRANTA

Granta Publications, 12 Addison Avenue, London W11 4QR

First published in Great Britain by Granta Books 2012

A CIP catalogue record for this book
is available from the British Library.

1 3 5 7 9 10 8 6 4 2

ISBN 978 1 84708 407 1

Typeset by M Rules
Printed and bound in Great Britain by
CPI Group (UK) Ltd, Croydon, CRO 4YY

To the memory of Brendan Jacobs (1920–2011)
and Tom Rae (1954–2011)

'... and he realized that the Magdalena, father of waters, one of the great rivers of the world, was only an illusion of memory.'

Gabriel García Márquez,
Love in the Time of Cholera

CONTENTS

Map   x

Prologue: The Writer Remembers   1

Part One: Distant Summer   11

Part Two: Upriver   71

Part Three: The Disappeared   153

Epilogue: Carnival   259

Further Reading   267

Acknowledgements   271

CARIBBEAN
SEA

PANAMA

Barranquilla

Cartagena

entrance : Hotel del Prado
Barranquilla

• Mompox

PACIFIC
OCEAN

basilica at
Yarumal

• Angostura

Yarumal •

RIO MAGDELENA

Medellin •

the square at Angostura, with
Saint Marianito portrait on bus
below: riders near San Agustín

C O L O M

RIO CAUCA

• Bogota

• Cali

• Popayan

• Páramo de las Papas

• San Agustin

ECUADOR

PERU

view of
Páramo de las Papas

manatees

VENEZUELA

Church of San Francisco, Mompox

Mutri's home at Mariquita

traditional bus

BIA

Rio Magdalena seen from hotel terrace at Puerto Berrio

Swamps near Mompox & Caiman below:
Petrol Refineries at Barrancabermeja

BRAZIL

Examples of carvings at San Agustin

THE WRITER REMEMBERS

I can still remember his eyes as they were late that night, full of spark at first, then alternately pensive, empty and tired, with the musicians playing on regardless, endlessly regaling the great writer with the *vallenatos* of his Caribbean youth. For a while I was sure he had fallen asleep. His head had long stopped nodding to the music, and his heavy eyelids appeared firmly shut. I remained sitting before him like a timid and over-awed acolyte, sweating from excitement and the heat. It was then that I noticed that he was not asleep at all. His eyes were half-open and staring quizzically towards me, wondering perhaps who I was. I felt for a few moments that I had turned into his younger self, while he had become a caiman watching me from the banks of a tropical river, somnolent and near invisible, but with eyes that peered above the murky waters, taking in everything.

I had seen him for the first time only the night before. It was January 2010, and a literary festival had just begun in the Colombian coastal town of Cartagena de Indias. People I met on the international festival circuit had been brought together with a large cross-section of Colombia's incestuous social elite. Any pretence at intellectual exchange had vanished by nighttime, when the brightly coloured colonial town revealed its hedonistic core in a near-continuous round of parties. The more hardened revellers usually ended up at the Bazurco Social Club, a celebrated nocturnal haunt in a district full of expats, prostitutes, budget tourists and lovers of the shabbily atmospheric.

I had gone there shortly before midnight. Drinkers were spilling out onto the street, sheltering from the fast, African rhythms of *champeta* that pounded from the high-ceilinged interior. I went inside. I wound my way past the erotically embraced dancers, squeezed through the jostling, beer-drinking students and reached the bar counter. A group of young publishers and journalists was gathered there in tight proximity, laughing and drinking rum. One of them, an English friend, told me to have a look at the back of the bar. 'You won't believe who's there,' he said with a drunken grin.

Among the faces of those seated at a long table at the back I recognized a Granadan poet, his best-selling novelist wife and a Madrid-based cultural commentator who had just brought out a book of literary memoirs entitled *Scrambled Egos*. And then I saw him, sitting next to the poet, but talking to no one, completely still, staring into the smoky space. The legendary Colombian writer.

His moustache was unmistakable, as were his receding thick curly hair, large glasses and dark, deep-set eyes. But my first thought on seeing this face almost as iconic for me as that of Che Guevara was that he was not the person everyone thought he was but rather a lookalike, an impersonator, someone who had been hired to lend a touch of parody to this literary occasion. He could have been one of those living statues who pose motionless for hours to attract the attention of shoppers and tourists. He moved barely at all, and then only when the inevitable admirers began shyly approaching him to ask for his signature, to express their devotion. Then his arm would jerk briefly into action, and a curt smile would appear on his face, as if a coin had been placed in a bowl in front of him.

His presence late at night in a popular bar was not, on reflection, particularly surprising. He was a man of the people, a lover of low life, a person with the grassroots appeal of a football star. What was remarkable was that he had finally come back to Cartagena. It was almost as if the Messiah had reappeared. Though he had a house in the colonial centre, he now barely moved from his adopted home in Mexico City. He notoriously avoided literary festivals, and had not been in Cartagena since 2006, when his arrival had created severe congestion of the old town's streets. He was now in his early eighties and had been seriously ill with cancer. I had heard various rumours about his imminent death.

However, the person sitting in the Bazurco Social Club

showed little sign of physical ill health, only of loneliness and a lack of connection with those whom he was with. Extreme fame had perhaps isolated him in his own world, turning him in old age into what his fiction predicted, the patriarch in autumn, the colonel to whom no one speaks, the general in his labyrinth, the embodiment of one hundred years of solitude. And then, as I continued looking at him, in furtive snatches across the crowded bar, I noticed something else. He had a look which I had observed so often in my elderly parents – a slightly angry and puzzled look, as if he wanted everyone around him to go away, as if he had become frighteningly aware that he had no idea who these people were and what he was doing in their company. My father had died of Alzheimer's in 1998, with no memory of his two children or of what he had done in his life. My mother, now weeks away from her ninetieth birthday, was in an advanced stage of dementia.

As I stood wondering whether the writer was going the same way as my parents, I considered going up to greet him, as so many others in the bar were now doing. The encounter, I suspected, would be as fleeting and meaningless as the touching of a holy relic, but at the very least I would be able to say afterwards that I had shaken hands with one of the giants of modern literature. An acquaintance from the festival handed me a bottle of beer, so I abandoned my plan. I rejoined the heavy drinkers at the bar counter. I doubted whether I would have a further opportunity to meet the writer.

But our paths would cross again the following night, at a party given by a Venezuelan millionaire at a boutique hotel in the tourist heart of the walled city. The guests were largely gathered on a roof terrace, dressed in smart cottons, sipping cocktails, taking in a vista of floodlit domes. The scene had the glamorous unreality of a rum advert, with the statutory quota of the bronzed and the beautiful. After a couple of hours or so, mainly listening to in-jokes and obscure literary gossip, I found myself alone with my thoughts, cut off from the general conversation, until a Moroccan novelist, who had briefly disappeared from our group, came back to join us, trembling with emotion. She had gone in search of a bathroom and had stumbled onto a small patio, where she had spotted the writer she referred to simply as '*him*'. He had just finished eating, and was surrounded by family and friends. A *vallenato* band was about to start. She was called over to his table. She had spoken to the man himself. 'He couldn't have been more approachable.'

Soon we were all downstairs, huddled awkwardly at a corner of the patio, talking among ourselves, listening to the *vallenatos*, pretending not to look at *him*, but waiting if only unconsciously for some sign or excuse to draw us into his circle. I identified his wife, one of his brothers and a rotund, angelic-faced friend of mine in charge of a foundation for journalists that the writer had created. During a pause in the music this friend, a much-loved local personality, with a hearty laugh, a forceful manner and an ability always to have his way without ever losing his charm, caught my eye, beckoned me over, rejected my shy protests and led me in front of the writer. 'Michael', he told him, 'is an Englishman obsessed by the river Magdalena.'

This was one of my friend's typical fanciful exaggerations,

based on my having once confided to him a vague scheme to head off one day towards the source of Colombia's longest river. My knowledge of the Magdalena was derived purely from books. I had devoured since childhood tales of South America's early explorers, to whom the Magdalena was the main point of entry into the continent's mysterious interior. But my developing interest in the river stemmed essentially from a passion for Colombia itself. I didn't visit the country until 2007, but I had had an immediate and uncanny sense of having known the place for most of my life, largely because it reminded me of the Spain with which I had fallen in love in my early teens.

I had steeped myself since then in Colombia's history and culture, the story of which was inseparable from that of the Magdalena. Not only did the river run right through the heart of the country, it had also served right up to the 1950s as the great artery of Colombia, the main thoroughfare for trade and travellers, the link between the diametrically opposed worlds of the coast and the Andes. And the more I read about the river, the more I thought of it as emblematic of the spirit of Colombia, and – by extension – all that I found fascinating, seductive, strange and disturbing about South America as a whole.

The Magdalena was a river of contradictions. It had inspired pioneering botanical studies, helped foster magical realism and given birth to some of the most exuberant music in the Latin world. It had also been the scourge of early travellers, the focus of Colombia's period of civil unrest known as *La violencia*, and the scene of so much deforestation and pollution that the river was now a notorious testimony to the destruction of the planet.

Whenever the subject of the Magdalena came up in conversation in Colombia, the response, tellingly, tended to veer between intense regret, nostalgia and longing. People dreamt of a period in the Magdalena's history when the river's beauty was untainted by violence and neglect. The elderly dwelt endlessly on the Magdalena of their youths.

The old writer sitting on the patio of the boutique hotel reacted to the mention of the river with a depth of feeling I had not expected. He burst into a smile, his eyes glowed and he held tightly to my wrist without seeming to want to let go. He looked up at his brother, like a child asking for a favour, and suggested that I be invited to their house, where he would love to talk to me at length about the Magdalena, the river of his life, the river that gave him the one reason for wanting to be young again. So that he could sail along it one more time.

The others who had come with me onto the patio, surprised at the attention the writer was giving me, were now advancing towards us, impatient to meet him themselves. One of them told him that his books had made her take up a life of literature; another introduced himself as the person responsible for the first Catalan translation of *One Hundred Years of Solitude*. The writer nodded solemnly without replying, continuing all the time to hold on to my wrist, waiting for the moment when he could go back to our conversation.

'I remember everything about the river, absolutely everything,' he eventually said, behaving as if there were no one else left on the patio, '... the caimans, the manatees ...'

The band returned, breaking into his reverie with the sounds of singing, accordions, maracas and drums. His grip on my hand tightened further as he insisted I stay with him to listen to the musicians, who, reading his thoughts, played a famous song about a man who changes into a caiman and sets off for the carnival at Barranquilla, at the mouth of the Magdalena. '... *Se va el caimán, se va el caimán, se va para Barranquilla*', they sang with an accelerating rhythm that soon had the writer rise to his feet and defy his old age with a lightening outburst of dance and joy.

Then he manoeuvred himself slowly back into his seat, exchanged handshakes and a few warm words with the musicians, and eventually became remote to everyone. The people I was with decided to go on to a bar in another part of town, but I stayed for the time being where I was, detained by the writer's wish that I should do so and by a hope that I would learn something else about him, if only by observing his eyes. I stayed for two more hours, until the music finally stopped and the writer and his family got up to leave. In a now weary tone, he said goodbye to me, and repeated the invitation to go and talk to him in his Cartagena home. The brother wrote out a number for me to ring.

I walked dazed and elated across the broad, open space separating the walled city from the shabbier district of Getsemaní. I caught up with my friends at around two in the morning, in a crammed, poky and deafeningly noisy bar called the Quiebracanto. I was desperate to tell someone about my encounter, about how kind and human the man was, how he appeared capable of seeing through people's pretentions and absurdities, and how he had the fundamental humility and simplicity I liked to believe was indicative of true greatness.

In the end I managed to attract the attention of a young group of Bogotá literati who had taken refuge from all the din and smoke on an outdoor wooden balcony. They were not particularly impressed by what I told them. 'You obviously got him on one of his more lucid days,' said a woman journalist known for her candid accounts of her complex love life. 'He'll probably have forgotten everything he said by tomorrow. He won't have any idea who you are.' The subject of his memory loss, according to her, was one that no one talked about in Colombia, for it was simply inconceivable that the great national icon should be suffering such a humiliating fate. 'Forget I told you,' she added, giving me one of her teasing smiles.

But I did not forget. Though I never saw him again (several calls to the number his brother gave me were not answered), I kept thinking back to that night in Cartagena and to what I had discovered. On my return to Europe, and to a mother losing all sense of reality, just as my father had done fifteen years earlier, I decided to reread *One Hundred Years of Solitude*. The novel acquired a deeper resonance in the light of what I had now learnt. Parts of the book I had once interpreted as reflections on a nation's ability to forget the past now seemed further examples of the author's extraordinary powers of premonition: the illness that makes the inhabitants of the imaginary village of Macondo lose their memories; the civil war that is fought for so long that neither side can remember what they are fighting for.

And I found new significance in the book's celebrated opening line, about a colonel, on the point of being executed, remembering the distant time when his father took him to discover ice. I could now imagine the colonel as the writer himself, nearing the end of his life, having forgotten almost everything about it, but still capable of dredging, from some obscure recess, memories full of magic, strangeness and wonder. I remembered him remembering the Magdalena.

'I remember everything about the river, absolutely everything ...' And, as I thought about these words, I remembered his eyes as they were later that night, when they had turned into those of a caiman, opening every so often to look at me in a way that made me imagine that nothing escaped their attention, that they could see right through me and read my thoughts, and that they were offering their blessing to a journey I had already begun that night in my mind, up a river that was also a metaphor of memory, into a luxuriant world of marvels and dangers, to areas of the past both brilliant and dark, on to the Magdalena's high and distant source, in Andean moorland, by the shores of oblivion.

PART ONE
DISTANT SUMMER

1

I was on my way at last to the Magdalena, in an airport lounge at Bogotá, in transit from Madrid, waiting for a delayed flight to the Caribbean port of Barranquilla. It was early evening, and dark, fast-moving clouds gave a sad and restless look to this high, mountain-walled city, making me think of the teenage García Márquez, newly arrived here after his life-changing first journey along the Magdalena and already pining for the perpetual summer of his coastal childhood.

Exactly a year had passed since my encounter with the writer in Cartagena, in the course of which my own yearning for the Caribbean world had become at times unbearably intense. A disturbing deterioration in my mother's dementia had led me continually to postpone my long-planned Magdalena quest. I had spent much of the year in a deeply introspective mood, searching for solutions for my mother, reflecting on her past, remembering my father, looking back to the time when I could never have imagined my parents' gradual loss of dignity and independence, when I knew nothing of the pathology of mental decline, when I had thought of memory as a source of mystery and awe.

My once high-flown notions of memory dated back to my adolescence, when I had been introduced to the multidisciplinary writings of a brilliant generation of cultural historians associated with London's Warburg Institute. One day I discovered Frances Yates' curious and compelling *The Art of Memory,* which traced the impact on the Middle Ages and Renaissance of an elaborate memory system evolved by the ancient Greeks. I was unable then to follow all of Yates' exceptionally involved and subtle argument. But I was taken by the idea of occult philosophers adapting for their own esoteric purposes a system that had originally been intended to have a purely practical application. I began to view memory as a key to an understanding of life's secrets.

I went on to spend much of my student years enclosed within the Warburg Institute, above whose entrance portal was inscribed the name of the ancient goddess of memory, Mnemosyne. The name became a daily reminder of memory as the central factor in our lives, the mother of the muses and the root of all knowledge. The sense of embarking on an intellectual adventure every time I entered the Institute was one that inspired in me early ambitions to become an academic.

These ambitions faded during the many years I researched a doctoral thesis. The academic world I had once perceived in terms of vast intellectual and imaginative range came to appear restrictive and petty. The exposure of my PhD supervisor and principal referee as a former Russian spy forced me finally into a decision I had already half taken. I took up a freelance life of writing and travelling. Combining the two activities meant I could explore academic subjects with the freedom and freshness I had so admired in the intellectual mentors of my schooldays.

My early travels were driven by a love of art and architecture, and by a wish to visit as many countries as possible. But, with time, I began to concentrate on Spain and Latin America, and to be guided less by objects than by an interest in people and nature. I started also to indulge in the idea of travel as a metaphorical progression akin to walking through one of the philosophical landscape gardens that had obsessed me when I was younger. I remembered visiting with my parents an Italian garden in which water from an upper spring was directed downhill into an expanding labyrinth of channels and ponds leading to a giant basin emblematic of the sea into which all lives flow.

The older I got the more I appreciated the role of travel as a stimulus to memories, and the way in which journeys even to new places were somehow always awakening memories of places seen in an ever-receding past. I was entering a phase of life in which my desire for travelling, far from being diminished, was acquiring a heightened urgency. Witnessing the decline of my parents was like a lesson to me, calling up a

Latin phrase as firmly embedded in my classically trained con-
sciousness as the name Mnemosyne: *carpe diem.*

By the time of my meeting with Gabriel García Márquez in
January 2010, Colombia had become the main focus of my
longing for distant travel. Its echoes of old Spain satisfied my
growing nostalgia, while the jubilance of its Caribbean world
appeared to me now like a necessary affirmation of life.
Though my mother's continuing insistence on living alone
made it impossible for me for the time being to consider
lengthy journeys away from Europe, I allowed myself a brief
return visit to Colombia in July. I had been invited there for
the celebrations marking the country's two hundred years of
independence from Spain.

These festivities coincided with the last days in power of
President Álvaro Uribe, who was keen to be remembered as
the man who brought stability to his country after two centuries of near-constant internal strife. As part of this public
relations exercise, I was flown by helicopter to a model indigenous village in the coastal range of the Sierra Nevada de Santa
Marta, where Uribe addressed the tribesmen with a talk about
how this terrestrial paradise had now been rid of all the guerrillas, paramilitaries and drug traffickers who had once
infested it. But the climax for me was climbing afterwards to
an isolated bird sanctuary, where a break in a torrential rain-
storm exposed at sunset an epic panorama of snow, jungle and
sea.

I caught in that moment my first glimpse of the Magdalena – as a faint glimmer of gold alongside the distant lights of

Barranquilla. The next morning, flying back to Bogotá from the coast, I saw the river again, and was able to follow its dark grey band from the waterlogged flatlands of its estuary into the enormously long valley dividing the eastern and central ranges of the Andes. Then the plane swerved away and the view below me was obliterated by clouds. Hidden beneath their blanket, somewhere to the south, lay the Magdalena's source. Though neither García Márquez, nor Colombia's early explorers, nor any of the travellers who had inspired my early interest in the river, had been to that place, I was resolved to do so myself. I envisaged the source as the ultimate goal of my forthcoming journey, as the mythical spring where Mnemosnye greeted travellers at the end of their lives.

My mother's condition deteriorated rapidly from July onwards, but my elder brother and I, perennial ditherers, were unsure as to what we should do about her. Numerous visits to doctors and hospitals did not solve this problem but at least gave me a better understanding of the physiology of memory. Memory, instead of being the complement to imagination and the soul, was now explained as a neatly ordered mechanism involving millions of neurons being triggered from different parts of the brain to produce specific types of memories: short-term, long-term, explicit, implicit, episodic and semantic.

Whereas my father's brain had been affected by protein abnormalities known as plaques and tangles, my mother's, I was told, was displaying the symptoms of normal vascular deterioration. In the continuing absence of a cure for dementia and Alzheimer's, a third of the world's population is expected to end up like her by the middle of this century.

Doctors assured my brother and I that we were doing
exactly the right thing in allowing our independent-minded
mother to continue staying in the house she had lived in for
over fifty years. However, this did not lessen our sense of a
crisis about to happen. We remained helpless onlookers watching her retreat into an ever more distorted version of her past.

Italian by birth, my mother had lived mainly in London since
marrying my Anglo-Irish father at the end of the Second World
War. She had been an actress in a Sicilian touring company
when they had first met, but had turned later into a housewife
of exceptionally rigid habits. For as long as I could remember
she had maintained a pudding-bowl hairstyle, together with a
weekly routine and timetable so unvarying that I knew, say,
that our clothes would be washed on Monday and stuffed pep-
pers served for supper on Sunday. She mistrusted spontaneity,
even when it came to entertainment, which was limited to
Saturday dinner parties, a Friday evening visit to the cinema or
theatre, an extremely reduced television diet (mainly nature
programmes, political debates and serializations of fictional
classics) and, above all, reading.

From five o'clock each afternoon she sat down in an armchair to read, her feet resting on a stool, her legs wrapped in
a blanket. She began with the newspaper (always the *Daily
Telegraph*) before moving on to a novel or memoir, or very
occasionally a biography. There were certain books she read
again and again, including Proust's *Remembrance of Things
Past*, parts of which she knew almost by heart. Many of her
other favourites were by Italian contemporaries of hers such as

Leonardo Sciascia, Primo Levi and Natalia Ginzburg, whose writings seem to have helped keep alive the memory of her itinerant Italian upbringing.

Though my mother ended up almost more fluent in English than in her native tongue, she continued to pepper her conversation with Italian phrases and family sayings of the kind that make up Natalia Ginzburg's quirky memoir, *Family Lexicon*. She also shared with Ginzburg a family full of eccentric North Italian relatives and ancestors. They would provide her with anecdotes to be brought up on every possible occasion.

Both my parents were incorrigible tellers of stories about themselves and their families. My brother and I, and even our friends, were subjected to stories we had heard hundreds of times before, but were always incapable of stopping, even if we muttered that we knew them already or displayed our obvious boredom. Moreover, the stories were taken from a repertoire that became increasingly restricted over the years, in line with the diminishing excitements in my parents' later lives. In my mother's case, the stories came to focus on a number of key incidents up to the time my brother and I were young children. The settings were invariably Italian.

Following the illness and death of my father, my mother's life became almost totally uneventful. She no longer invited anyone to dinner, hated having her routines spoilt by people dropping by to see her, and restricted her inessential outings in London to an occasional visit to the theatre. More than ever she took refuge in the world of her books and memories.

Then suddenly her memories started failing and she became

gradually incapable of reading. Up to the age of eighty-six, she had remained a beautiful and self-contained woman, capable of living on her own, not needy of outside stimulus, always elegantly dressed, in perfect health and looking much younger than her years. Had she died then, peacefully in her sleep, after an evening with one of her children, she would have had good reason to be contented. But the perfect construct she had tried to make of her life would from that point onwards be completely undermined.

The first symptom of her mental decline was paranoia. She thought that the Filipino cleaner she had reluctantly taken on was stealing from her. She sacked the cleaner, employed another one, got rid of her as well, and then decided to do all the housework herself, which made her more tired than ever and consequently more prone to the fits of violent anger and hysteria that heralded the second phase of her condition, and which were usually followed by brief moments of sadness and contrition, and the realization that the remarkable self-control which had hitherto held her life together, and enabled her to maintain a polite facade in front of others, was disappearing.

'I'm not going mad, I'm not going mad,' she said repeatedly, as she began to lose everything, her keys, her jewellery, her hearing, her rationality, her clothes, her peace of mind, her desire to live. She said she would kill herself if only she knew how, and asked me if boot polish would do the trick.

Soon she was sensing strange presences in the house, entertaining an imaginary man for breakfast, saying goodbye to my dead father before he set off for work, looking inside her sons' former bedroom in search of the children she had known as 'the boys'. 'The boys went out early this morning and have not returned!', she would ring to tell me in a panic, and I would have to remind her that I was in fact one of the boys and I was perfectly safe and sound, but I was worried about her and she shouldn't continue living on her own. 'There's nothing wrong with me!', she would shout, slamming down the phone.

Her diminishing, episodic memories revealed deep traumas and underlying guilt: she constantly relived the moment when she was heavily pregnant with me and had been spun under-water by a giant wave; she talked about having killed my father by sending him in his last few months to live in a home.

She clearly feared more than anything what she had done to my father. She could not bear the idea of living with anyone other than her children. She kicked out all the day-time carers I sent to look after her, and tried holding on as hard as she could to her strict domestic routines of the past half century. She even maintained her habit of sitting down to read, even though she would stare endlessly at the same page, taking in almost nothing. She was existing mainly on implicit memo-ries, the memories that enable you to function without thinking.

In an attempt to unearth the happy memories from her past I sat down with her to leaf through family photo albums of the last sixty years. I found then further confirmation of what I had come to notice more and more in the course of 2010: that my mother had lost virtually all remaining sense of time and place. She looked at photos taken on an Italian beach in 1955 and thought they were of a recent holiday. She looked at photos of her North London home, my brother's Italian

Alpine retreat and the Spanish village where I had mainly been living in recent years, and thought they were all the same country.

She turned out to have no clear idea of where she was, or who I was, other than knowing that her house was pleasingly familiar and I was someone she loved. In the end she decided I was her husband. 'Oh look, there you are,' she said, pointing to a beach shot in which I appeared as a curly-headed toddler, except she was not pointing to me at all but to my handsome thirty-year-old father, who was holding me in his arms.

That I was being mistaken in my late fifties for my young father was difficult at first for me to take in, and also resulted in much jealousy on my mother's part, after I kept on disappearing abroad, and going home nightly to another woman ('Can't you see how insulting that is?', she would say). But the delusion had at least one positive effect. My father, who had gradually slipped from my thoughts since his death from Alzheimer's at the age of seventy-six, returned to shadow me.

He had been a kind, generous but distant father, with whom I had only known any degree of intimacy when his memory was already failing. After suffering several years of insecurity in the aftermath of the war, he had settled down to a stable job as a company lawyer for Shell, earning large sums of money, but coming home always late and distracted, with little time other than for my mother, whom he unreservedly adored and with whom he never quarrelled. The sense of exclusion I sometimes felt in London generally disappeared during family holidays, when I had glimpses of what was perhaps my father's true self, or at least what he had been like before being constrained by his work and my mother's draconian routines. He became the person whom I had heard described by some of his university friends, someone open to any challenge, driven by passionate instincts and prone to fits of mad dancing. Seeing García Márquez rise so joyously to his feet that night in Cartagena had brought back one of my most recurring memories of my father – a memory of him breaking into a joyous sprint on the racecourse at Epidaurus, until being told off by my mother, who said that at his age he should be more careful, because such sudden pressure on the heart could easily be dangerous.

For all my father's apparent contentment with life, he must have been constantly beset by frustrations. Probably his greatest regret was not to have pursued until it was too late the literary ambitions he had harboured since his teens. His years at Shell brought him recognition in his field of law, a good salary and even an OBE. But he longed all the time to give up his job and devote himself to writing. In his late fifties, after much less experienced colleagues had been promoted above him, he finally decided he had had enough. He retired early, to become immersed in the first of several projects he had been thinking about for ages.

He already had a name as a writer of lucid and concise legal reports. He believed that these skills would be sufficient to write a book bringing together what he regarded as the ordinary thoughts of an ordinary man. He was self-deluded enough to think that anyone would want to read such a work, let alone publish it. He was indignant that not even my mother showed the slightest interest in the project during its years of gestation. He was heartbroken by the dozens of curt letters of rejection he eventually received. Yet he was soon enthusiastically engaged in another project, similarly doomed to failure – a book based on the correspondence of his railway-building father. Finally, encouraged largely by me, he wrote the work which he had wanted more than any other to write – a memoir of his years as an intelligence officer for the British Army in Italy.

I had not expected by this stage a literary masterpiece, but rather some honest account for the benefit of his children and grandchild of what had obviously been the key years of his life. I had also envisaged an interesting historical document that would complement his army colleague Norman Lewis's celebrated *Naples '44*. But the manuscript I was shown turned out to be unrevealing, clumsily written and lacking all perception and emotion. I would realize only in retrospect that his mind had been affected by Alzheimer's.

His memoir would probably not have been written at all had it not been for a lifelong habit whose true significance was at last beginning to dawn on me. Every evening since at least his teens he had tried setting aside time for the keeping of a diary. Over the years he had accumulated diaries amounting to thousands of pages, all of which he had placed in folders and chronologically filed away. I began now to suspect that he had had an intuition of future memory loss from an early age and had written down and methodically stored his daily musings and activities in anticipation of the day when his entire life would appear as a blur.

After my father's death, I resisted for a long while taking a proper look at his private papers, daunted by their sheer bulk and by a handwriting almost as difficult to decipher as my own. But, late in 2010, when much of my time in London was being spent in my mother's house, I distracted myself by searching through my father's filing cabinets. I was hoping to uncover some spark of literary talent from my father's distant past. I almost gave up after reading a couple of overblown, autobiographical short stories, but when I came to the diaries themselves I was taken by surprise. They displayed a fluency and emotion entirely absent from his later attempts to summarize them. In following my father from a dreary army barracks outside Winchester to the exotic colours and brilliant sunlight of Sicily, I felt as if I too had embarked upon a journey of enormous importance. A journey to discover a man I barely knew.

The year was almost over. My mind was somewhere between wartime Sicily, present-day Colombia and the unlocatable world that was my mother's. I was sitting on a sofa in front of her, immersed in a leather-bound diary of 1943 while occasionally watching my mother as her eyes moved repeatedly up and down the same page of the newspaper.

She was no longer living on her own. A series of near explosions in the kitchen, followed by a serious fall from bed, gave her little choice than to accept a full-time carer. To my surprise, she raised no objections. She had emerged from the hell of half-knowing what was happening to her and was now at the more contented stage of not apparently knowing anything at all. Her improved situation enabled me to consider more seriously the prospect of a long journey up the Magdalena. I went ahead and bought a ticket for Barranquilla for early in the new year.

Then other problems surfaced. Colombia was still suffering from 'La Niña', a cyclical weather phenomenon causing devastating rains that were now predicted to last throughout the supposed dry season between January and March. Massive flooding in the Magdalena estuary had already left an estimated two million people homeless and water pouring down the river at a rate of 18,000 cubic metres a second.

A friend from Cali wrote to say that I had probably chosen the worst time in a hundred years to sail up the Magdalena. According to him, I not only ran the risk of being drowned or trapped for weeks, but I was also unlikely to find a boat willing to take me anywhere. For good measure he added that the security situation along the valley was no longer as rosy as the Colombian government was claiming. Guerrillas were still active along the upper reaches of the river, and former paramilitary units were regrouping as drug-smuggling gangs such as the notorious *Águilas Negras*, 'The Black Eagles'.

I had no intention of abandoning my Magdalena journey, but worries about the dangers I might imminently be facing lingered as I sat on my mother's sofa, trying to lose myself in my father's adventures in Sicily.

I had got to the part when he was summarizing his first impressions of the land that would change his life, a place badly scarred by the war, unbearably hot, mosquito-ridden, corrupt and impoverished, but with an uncommonly welcoming people and an atmosphere heavy with sexual promise.

I paused soon afterwards. My mother, who noticed the tiniest details, down to the slightest mark on my clothes, was looking straight at me. 'Is there anything wrong?' she asked, detecting a watery sadness in my eyes. 'Nothing at all,' I cheerily replied, knowing I could never now convey to her the full pathos and bathos of the line I had just read in my father's diary. 'I have a deep inner conviction', noted the 21-year-old soldier, 'that I shall rise to considerable prominence as a writer.'

2

And finally I was in Barranquilla, late at night, in a taxi with a dark-haired woman whom I had met earlier that day on the plane from Madrid. She was called Marcela, and was returning to her home city. She had been living in Spain for the past few years, but was not happy there, especially not in Madrid, where she hated the cold winters and the unwelcoming people who did not return her warm smile when she greeted them in the street, or else interpreted the smile in a way she had not intended. 'In Barranquilla', she stressed, 'we smile at everyone. It does not have any other meaning.'

I noticed the transformation she had undergone in the course of the journey, her manner becoming more open and relaxed with the necessary adjustment of clothing as we travelled from a sub-zero Madrid to a grey and windy Bogotá, and now to a sweltering Barranquilla, where she had been reduced to a light cotton dress in brilliant yellow. 'I become a very different person whenever I'm here,' she said as we drove from the airport towards the centre of a city regularly described as having no obvious centre, no distinguishing monuments and indeed nothing to merit a tourist visit other than its famous carnival. 'You're going to love Barranquilla,' she beamed.

'Of course, you have to be careful,' she continued, as the interminable straight road we had been on for the past twenty minutes entered a poorly lit sprawl of low-rise dwellings eroded and blackened by humidity. 'There are parts of the city I wouldn't visit at night. There are some areas you shouldn't even visit by day, especially if you're a gringo.' The worst districts, apparently, were those that bordered the Magdalena. When she was last in the city, visiting an aunt who lived near the river, she had been on a bus that had been held up by an hysterical gunman.

'I don't want to frighten you,' she insisted, before alarming me further with a story of the lingering presence of paramilitaries in the outlying villages in the Magdalena basin. A colleague of hers from one of these villages, a fellow teacher, was told by paramilitaries not to travel to Barranquilla, even though her mother was seriously ill in hospital there. She disobeyed them. They intercepted the van she was travelling on and took her off it. She was never seen again.

The urban landscape remained unchanging, intersected by a grid of dusty streets that were said by Marcela to become like rivers at times of heavy rain. The taxi-driver agreed, telling us that this whole area of the city had been a near swamp only a couple of weeks ago.

'Every year it's the same old story,' he added. 'Some years, like this year, it rains more than normal. But every year there's flooding, and the government does nothing about it. It's been dry now since Christmas, and that's all that seems to matter.' 'That's so typical of Colombia,' butted in Marcela. 'We don't think ahead, we immediately forget the past. This is a country of forgetting.'

Barranquilla's historic centre was soon upon us, no less dark and menacing than the districts we had gone through, but with boarded-up warehouses and an incongruous touch of elegance in the shape of a newly painted colonial customs house in vivid blue. Then we left the main street, to be confronted a few minutes later by a gaudy version of Big Ben illuminated by oscillating coloured lights. Almost imperceptibly we had entered one of the smarter parts of the city, a jumble of shops, internet cafes and untidy rows of villas and gardens climaxing in what could have been Hollywood.

'Your hotel,' announced Marcela as we drove into the flood-lit grounds of a neo-baroque palace in bright cream stucco. A porter with a top hat and a gold-braid jacket was waiting under a spacious portico. I had booked into Barranquilla's oldest hotel for my first nights in the city, but I had not expected anything as grand as this. 'The appearance is slightly deceptive,' commented Marcela, who was staying on in the taxi, 'but the hotel certainly has character.' A bellboy took me into a marbled vestibule resonant with ghosts.

The Hotel El Prado was like a tunnel leading back into the past. It was built in the 1930s as Colombia's first tourist hotel.

It had a palm-shaded courtyard with a swimming pool, chandeliers everywhere, a mahogany lift operated by a lift boy, and corridors with black-and-white chequered floors that enhanced an illusion of infinite recession. In the 1980s and early Nineties, when Barranquilla had threatened to turn into a Chicago of gangland crime, the place had been owned by a notorious drug trafficker, Sheila Arana de Nasser. After her arrest in 1994, the hotel had been taken over by the state, who appeared to have done little to it. The rooms were grand but malfunctioning, and the immense size of the place, I had heard, was only justified at carnival time, when prices quadrupled and vacancies were non-existent.

But, as Marcela had said, the place had character. I imagined it was like one of the abandoned luxury buildings where my father had been billeted in Sicily. Its state of gentle neglect enhanced its evocativeness, recalling Barranquilla's heyday in the 1930s and Forties, when navigation on the Magdalena had flourished as never before, drawing settlers from all over Colombia, expanding yet more the city's population of immigrants from Syria, Lebanon, Palestine, France, Germany, Italy, China, Japan.

The writer Christopher Isherwood had stayed in the hotel at a turning point in Colombia's history. I thought of him on my first night here, as I slouched half-asleep in the almost empty courtyard bar. He was here in September 1947, waiting for a boat to take him on the first stage of a six-month journey through South America. He was increasingly fed up with Barranquilla, and did not appreciate the lack of hot water in his bedroom. He spent much of his time lounging in the hotel's public spaces, staring at the plants, the palms and the pool. One day someone pointed out to him a prominent socialist politician predicted to be Colombia's next president, Jorge Eliécer Gaitán.

The image of Gaitán sitting on one of the chairs around me was yet another reminder of the way Colombia's tragic past is never far from the surface. Less than a month after Isherwood's return to America Gaitán was assassinated in the capital, Bogotá. The event brought to a head Colombia's eternal conflict between Liberals and Conservatives. It sparked off the bloody riots known as the *Bogotazo*, which in turn led to the period defined with chilling simplicity as *La violencia*. The violence, perpetuated by Army and guerrillas alike, veered apocalyptically out of control from the 1980s onwards with the mushrooming activities of paramilitary groups formed for the supposed defence of citizens.

Even as I switched my thoughts to the boat on which Isherwood eventually travelled, I could not help thinking about Colombia's tragedies. The *David Arango* was the largest, most luxurious and most successful passenger boat ever to have navigated the Magdalena. It was the boat that took the fifteen-year-old García Márquez on his life-changing first journey up the river in 1943. And it continued running throughout the 1950s, when the country was sinking into chaos and the river beginning to lose much of its traffic. However, in March 1961, while moored outside the town of Magangué, it caught fire and was turned in a matter of hours into a metal shell. The disaster left its mark on the Colombian psyche. For García Márquez the burning of the *David Arango* was the ultimate metaphor for a childhood which could not be recovered. For Colombia it meant the end of the Magdalena as the main means of passenger transport into the interior.

The river's subsequent fate came to be mirrored in the decline of the Hotel El Prado, whose intimidating corridors provided me with a final challenge before I collapsed exhausted into bed.

When I woke up disoriented and troubled the next morning, I was still uncertain how I would travel up the Magdalena. During the dreaming stage of the journey I had vague ideas about hiring launches, making friends with fishermen, practising my rowing, and using the only form of public river transport that survived, a speedy, reputedly dangerous and purely local small craft called a *chalupa*. Then the floods had come and, for a while, I thought my only feasible option would be to persuade the Colombian Navy to take me on one of their rescue ships.

The Navy did not reply to my enquiries, but in the meantime the floods subsided, and I heard about the irregular cargo services that still laboriously plied the river, running the risk of getting stuck for days on a sandbank during the dry season. Travelling on such a boat would be the closest approximation to river journeys as García Márquez had known them, slow and sociable, with far broader views than on a lower vessel and time enough to study every subtle change in the Magdalena's mood.

A journalist friend in Cartagena put me in touch with NAVESCO, a company describing itself as 'dedicated to the international maritime transport of solid bulk cargoes'. I received a warm response from the head of the company's Barranquilla branch, Juan Alberto Montoya. He said he would try his best to get me onto a boat. He also offered to send a 'driver whom I could trust' to take me to his office on my first morning in the city. He conveyed efficiency and a sense of urgency at odds with my stereotypical view of the laid-back Caribbean world.

The car turned up shortly after 7 a.m., interrupting my breakfast of tropical fruits served under a palm tree. Sunlight and the early morning drive through the city cleared away some of the more disturbing thoughts I had been having since my arrival. Structures that had appeared grim and threatening by night were revealed by day to be enlivened by an uncontrollable exuberance of vegetation, graffiti, posters and spontaneous splashes of ornament. There was a joy and sensuality to all the chaos. I wanted to dance.

Juan Alberto's office was in shady surroundings on the city's outskirts. A digital sign in the reception area read 'Welcome Mr Michael Jacobs'. Juan Alberto, a boyish fifty-year-old with glasses, kept me waiting for barely a minute.

A lavish coffee-table book about the Magdalena was sitting on his desk and he excitedly leafed through it, showing me the beauty spots he had always wanted to visit himself. He said that what I intended to do was the unfulfilled aspiration of most Colombians. He appeared pleased for a while just to chat, about my interest in the Magdalena, about Colombia in general.

He talked about the great differences in attitude between the Colombians from the coast and those from the mountainous interior, the *costeños* and the *cachacos*. The latter secretly envied the proverbially relaxed and informal *costeños*, but the *cachacos* had a reputation for getting things done, and had galvanized the industries and large-scale businesses of the coast. He himself, unsurprisingly, was a *cachaco*. He was from the Andean city of Medellín, where he knew a doctor who had studied the unusually high incidence of early onset Alzheimer's in a cluster of villages above the Magdalena Valley.

'But let's not talk too much about that as we'll forget what you've come here for,' he joked, as we got down to business. The first priority, as far as he was concerned, was for me to acquire a Colombian cellphone. He sorted this out by phoning the local director of the telephone company with the 'finest coverage along the Magdalena'. Then there was the matter of finding me a boat. He said he had left this in the hands of a transport company with whom NAVESCO regularly collaborated, the Naviera Fluvial Colombiana. He was still waiting to hear back from them.

For the past fifty years the Naviera Fluvial Colombiana had dominated cargo transport along the Magdalena with the use of what he referred to as a *remolcador*, a type of tugboat capable of pushing up to a dozen or so giant barges, laden mainly with goods going to and from the petrol refinery at Barrancabermeja, about halfway up the river. Though NAVESCO had pioneered boats capable of defeating one of the main hurdles of upstream navigation, Barranquilla's low-arched Pumarejo Bridge, these particular vessels went no further than the diminutive port of Puerto Pinsa, a couple of miles from his office. He asked if I wanted to go there.

Five minutes later we were driving along a tree-lined dust track running between swamps. An iguana slipped off the road as we passed, while overhead flew what Juan Alberto identified as a flock of *gallinazos* or 'giant hens', the local word for 'vultures'. The landscape felt suddenly remote from Barranquilla and so far from anywhere that I almost envisaged stumbling across a caiman or a manatee. But my mention of these animals produced a momentary introspectiveness in Juan Alberto, as if I had touched on a problem which even he was incapable of solving. 'They've almost all gone today from the Magdalena,' he sighed.

We reached the port, where I had my first close-to sight of a river described by the eighteenth-century German explorer Alexander von Humboldt as 'grandiose and majestic'. Juan Alberto, sharing some of my thrill at seeing its muddy waters expand to the horizon under a clear morning light, made an observation I would hear again and again over the coming days. He spoke about Barranquilla as a city which owes everything to the river and yet turns its back on it. He thought that few other cities so neglect their river, hiding it behind the worst slums or at the end of tracks like the one we had just been on. He paused for a moment, as if searching for a reason for this. Fear of the river's destructive powers? A desire to forget its terrible history?

The call from the Naviera Fluvial Colombiana finally came through. I was told I had to get there at twelve o'clock to meet up with one of its directors, Hector Cruz. Juan Alberto assured me that I was now almost certain of getting a boat, and that the meeting would turn into a lunch and then into an afternoon of lavish hospitality and conversation. 'I know what those people are like, they're a danger,' he smiled.

Hector Cruz greeted me at a slickly modernized office in front of the city's old customs house. He had a studious, put-upon look. He was courteous but somewhat evasive, and understandably anxious to get back to more important work than looking after an Englishman with funny ideas about the Magdalena. With minimal preliminaries he told me that the Naviera Fluvial Colombiana would be delighted to have me as their guest and they wanted me to travel on the latest and most luxurious of their *remolcadores*, which was named after the company's nonagenarian founder, Humberto Muñoz.

My main concern up to now had been to start the journey before the return of La Niña's heavy rains. At least, I thought, I was going to be spared the usual dry season worries about sandbanks. But I had underestimated the Magdalena's extraordinary capriciousness. Despite the floods before Christmas, the river had diminished so rapidly since then that the journey upstream to Barrancabermeja was going to take me at least ten days and probably more. And if the water level continued dropping at the current rate, Hector foresaw major problems. I now appeared to be in a race against both rains and drought.

'Anything else you want to know?' asked Hector, closing a file in which he had noted that I wanted to leave Barranquilla as soon as possible. I asked about my options for continuing upstream from Barrancabermeja. 'Take a plane,' he answered firmly. 'Of course there are buses and small boats, but I wouldn't recommend these. We're talking about parts of Colombia where there is absolutely no tourism. As a solitary gringo you're bound to raise suspicions.'

I said I thought that Colombia had changed beyond recognition in recent years, and that the Magdalena Valley had long ago lost its reputation as the most dangerous place in the world. But Hector was not really listening.

'Look,' he announced, putting an end to the conversation, 'the company can guarantee your safety up to Barrancabermeja, but not afterwards. Our boats always carry soldiers. If you want to go any further up the river, my advice is to get yourself a Colombian companion.'

As he got up to say goodbye, he promised to phone me when he had more news about my passage. I slipped in a request to talk to Humberto Muñoz himself, whom Juan Alberto had described as a most engaging old man with an unparalleled knowledge of the river. Hector said Señor Muñoz was ill and in Bogotá, but if I wanted he could get me a copy of the man's recently published autobiography.

Instead of the convivial, protracted lunch I had been looking forward to, I spent a solitary hour reading Humberto Muñoz's *The Magdalena: My Life*. It was a tale of a cachaco's obsessive love of Barranquilla and the river, beginning with the author's stay in the Hotel El Prado in 1941 and continuing with a passionate affair with a sensual Cuban woman whom he met that year on the *David Arango*. The river had brought Muñoz enormous fame and financial success. But his family, whom he compared to the Kennedy clan in America, seems to

have been cursed. Four of his children had been killed in circumstances he did not disclose. I preferred for the moment not
to know what had happened to them. I was trying to steady
my nerves.

I waited to hear from Hector. And, while waiting, I began to
enjoy Barranquilla's mounting pre-Carnival atmosphere. The
Carnival was six weeks away, but numerous pre-Carnival parties were being held and the first Carnival decorations were
going up. Masks had started appearing on walls, grotesque
effigies could be found slumped on office chairs, and columns
and trees had already been wrapped with tinsel and coloured
streamers.

    After a couple of days in Barranquilla I moved to a more
modest hotel flanked by gaudily decorated miniature palms. I
had come round to accepting that my stay in the city was
likely to be lengthier than expected, but I no longer minded so
much. I was becoming pleasantly ensnared by Barranquilla.
'You should be careful, you know,' said a Barranquillero to
whom I got talking at a Carnival club near my new hotel.
'Barranquilla has that effect on people. My father came here
from Paris for a few days and stayed a lifetime. I can think of
numerous cases like his.'

    He told me about an article on the city written by one such
person, a friend of García Márquez with the sonorous name of
Plinio Apuleyo Mendoza. Mendoza, playing on Barranquilla's
position at the mouth of a river, defined his adopted home as
a place that 'digests everything it receives'. He also likened the
city to a calmly flowing stream that presents no challenges to

those carried along with it. 'That's why García Márquez had to tear himself away from the place before it was too late,' said my Barranquillero acquaintance. 'He adored Barranquilla, more than any other city, but he needed conflict in his life, otherwise he wouldn't have got anywhere.'

I nodded sympathetically, but the club was not the best place to listen to subtleties, certainly not at this time of night, with so many sights and other sounds competing for my attention: the pirouetting transvestite at the door, the Afro-Caribbean band setting up in a back room, the primary-coloured clothes, the copious glasses of rum, the shrieks and laughs of friends greeting each other for perhaps the first time since last year's Carnival. The essence of Barranquilla seemed to have been distilled into this rambling, frayed villa that was now the headquarters of the Carnival group with the suitably anarchic name of *Disfrázate como Quieras* ('Dress As You Please').

I had been introduced to the group by the cherubic-faced friend who had presented me to García Márquez the year before, Jaime Abello. He wanted me to get to know them so that, on my return from the Magdalena journey ('should you ever return'), I could experience the Carnival as part of a dancing, day-long procession through the streets of Barranquilla. My dancing, I protested, was wild and without rhythm, just like my father's had been and my grandfather's before him. 'That doesn't matter,' said Jaime. 'Just dance how you want to dance.'

I met some of my potential Carnival companions, a lesbian blogger with a bowler hat, a museum director in lederhosen, a French human rights activist constantly swaying her hips, a kindly old anthropologist with an indigenous shawl, a film star who had just posed for a magazine article illustrating the sensuality of the mature woman. After several glasses of rum I found myself caught up in a surreal flow of impressions waiting to cohere.

Then, within this apparent randomness, a unifying factor began to emerge. Everyone I spoke to had some close connection with the Magdalena: one person was organizing a major conference on the river's future; another was the child of parents who had met on a steamboat; several others were the descendants of the river's leading engineers and entrepreneurs. The biggest surprise came while talking to the film star's husband, a towering man with jet-black hair tied in a ponytail and the look of a Caribbean buccaneer. His name was Owen Jones. I had read all about an ancestor of his who had come out from Wales in the 1850s to begin the annual dredging of the river. I now heard that his family was still employed in the task. Owen joked that when the Colombian government managed finally to clean up the river he would be out of business.

The band was now in full swing and one of their dancers was distracting me with a mesmerizingly frenetic and sinuous routine with a hat. A young composer, Luis Fernando Franco, chose this moment to introduce himself. He had overheard some of my conversation with Owen and was wondering whether my interest in the Magdalena extended to the river's songs and dances, an apparently endless repertoire. 'Every family along the river has its musician,' he stressed. 'It must be the most musical river in the world.'

Owen's wife started to dance, followed by her husband and almost everyone else in the room, but Luis had hooked me with his talk about the Magdalena's musical traditions, which he was currently researching and would probably be doing for many years to come. Tonight's musicians were all friends of his. They were villagers from the Magdalena who had been displaced by *La violencia* to Barranquilla, the city that digested everything, the city which had mixed together melodies of Spanish origin, African rhythms, indigenous dances, to create the music that was now uniting everyone on the dance floor, *la cumbia*.

During a brief lull in the music, Luis had a word in the lead singer's ear, then commanded the room to silence. A special piece of music was going to be played for my benefit. It opened with a recitative. The singer's unaccompanied words, harsh, plaintive and rapidly rising in volume, were devoted to the Magdalena, the 'river of our lives', a lost Andean stream destined to become the artery of Colombia, and then the nation's soul, a rush of emotions and memories heading towards their release, in the sea near Barranquilla, '*donde nace la cumbia*' ('where cumbia is born'). 'DONDE NACE LA CUMBIA,' he shouted again as loud as he could, inciting an explosion of maracas, flutes and drums, a great cheer from the room and a frenzied contortion of limbs.

3

The following afternoon I received a message on my newly acquired Colombian cellphone. A date for my departure had been fixed. The *Humberto Muñoz* would be setting sail from Barranquilla on 5 February.

I was reclining at the time in a luxurious flat on the city's periphery, skimming through the wordy epilogue to a massive compilation of historical texts about the Magdalena. 'The Magdalena', wrote its author in 1958, 'is today merely a shadow of its former self. Ravaged by the sordid roar of tug-boats, with their containers of diesel, its sorry appearance today should shame all Colombians.'

The apartment's owner, Gustavo Bell, came back into his minimalist sitting-room with a large jug of fruit juice. An eminent historian of the Caribbean with an engagingly informal and youthful manner, Gustavo had also been Governor of the

Magdalena Province and Vice-President of Colombia. 'As an historian in Colombia you have to take on the most unlikely jobs,' he laughed as he sat down in front of me, next to a bronze statuette of the Magdalena's most enduring legend, *el hombre caimán*, the man who turns into a caiman.

I told him the news about my passage on a tugboat. He said he couldn't think of a more romantic way to travel along the river. 'The boats even have something of the look of the old steamships,' he said of these once much-derided vessels. He added that if it hadn't been for the tugboats, and in particular the singular determination of Humberto Muñoz and the Naviera Fluvial Colombiana, the Magdalena would be in an even worse state than it was.

Why had the Colombian government allowed the river to become like this? Gustavo, as a good diplomat and politician, sidestepped the question. He talked instead about the historical roots of the Magdalena's deterioration. He talked about the days when the river ran through uninterrupted jungle, and how Humboldt had predicted that deforestation would have devastating effects not just on the river but on the planet as a whole.

By the mid-nineteenth century, as the landscape became progressively barer, the river began silting up alarmingly, necessitating the calling-in of foreign hydraulic experts. A French engineer of the 1880s concluded that mineral residues flowing into the river from Colombia's mines were largely to blame. He thought that something more drastic than regular dredging needed to be done. Nothing was.

Heavy industries, rapid urbanization and the consequent

uncontrolled release of waste and sewage into the river, compounded the Magdalena's decline into the river it was today – 'an open drain, albeit still a very enticing drain'.

Gustavo urged me to step out onto his balcony, one of the few places in the city with a good view of the river. An invigorating wind was blowing, clearing the haze and brightly exposing the much-feared Boca de Cenizas, the hazardous inlet where the Magdalena reaches the sea. I noticed even at this distance how rough the waters were. A long line of rocks had been laid out to sea in the 1920s to try and break the impact of the waves and protect the river's mouth. With the aid of a pair of binoculars I was able to see that this pencil-thin line was dotted with precarious homes made from driftwood and scrap. From one of the more privileged dwellings in Barranquilla I was looking out towards what were probably the poorest.

Ever since coming to Barranquilla I had been trying to reach Boca de Cenizas. The train that had once gone there had been permanently suspended after the recent floods, and the excursionists who had braved the journey in an open horse-drawn carriage had suffered a number of assaults. In any case I wanted to experience the place just as the first Europeans had done, by boat. Juan Alberto Montoya, my self-appointed guardian angel in Barranquilla, had been trying his best to organize a trip with one of the pilots who guided oceangoing vessels into the city's harbour. But, he warned, this was not the safest time of year for such a trip. It was the season of the *brisas*. The threat of 'breezes' did not seem particularly frightening, but then I learnt that *brisas* in Colombian Spanish had the stronger meaning it had had in Golden Age Spain: gale-force winds.

'I hope you have a strong stomach and a good sense of balance,' said Juan Alberto when he phoned to say that he had found the right pilot for me, someone not only prepared to risk taking on a passenger, but also with a reputation as one of the most fearless and skilful pilots in Barranquilla today. He arranged for the three of us to meet up that night for supper, together with a retired sea captain with a passion for navigational history. His chosen venue was a legendary bar and restaurant frequented by the young García Márquez when his novel *One Hundred Years of Solitude* was already in embryo.

La Cueva proved a disappointment. Promoted as a 'living memory of Colombia's cultural past', it was a piece of fossilized bohemia that sanctified and mythologized frivolous moments that should have remained purely ephemeral: the footprint of the circus elephant with which a painter had once tried to enter the establishment; the two bullet holes fired by a writer into a friend's canvas after his beer had been pissed into. But I liked the idea of García Márquez's spirit being somehow present in the background, keeping an eye on me. I also took immediately to my new companions.

The two men, Alejandro Henao and Captain Ricardo Moreno, were opposites in personality. The handsome Alejandro, the pilot, projected optimism and physical confidence, and was someone to whom I was happy to entrust my life. He had come from Medellín to Barranquilla in his early twenties and now never wanted to leave the city. He had a more intense love for his job than anyone I had ever met before. He insisted that he would choose to work as a pilot even if no one paid him to do so.

Captain Ricardo, a wiry, distinguished old man with a white stubble of a beard, had a smile both mischievous and sad. Witty, sophisticated and cosmopolitan, he was a mix of French, Colombian and American blood, but considered his true fatherland to be the sea. He was full of stories about his maritime past, particularly about his childhood in the nearby former seaport of Puerto Colombia. As a thirteen-year-old he had braved sharks while propelling a home-made raft. However, he had reached an age when he viewed the world he had once loved with disillusionment. Unlike Gustavo Bell, he did not hold back when it came to expressing criticism of the incompetence, corruption and apathy of successive Colombian governments.

'The politicians in Bogotá have barely a clue as to what's going on in the rest of the country. They're only interested in elections and keeping people happy with carnivals. Everyone in Colombia merely obeys orders without questioning them. No one gives a thought to the future. One day there'll be no one left on the planet.'

His portrait of Caribbean Colombia today was bleak. Under continuing threat from 'the worst piracy in the world', it was now also on the verge of a chemical-induced catastrophe. Chemicals used on land were penetrating the soil to the extent that animals were dying and agriculture would soon be destroyed. The chemicals that were being thrown into the

Magdalena were having a still more noticeable impact. They were being washed into the sea and destroying all the corals, the extinction of which was wrecking the marine ecosystem and leaving the Caribbean beaches unprotected from soil erosion and flooding.

He asked me if I had read García Márquez's essay *The Magdalena: The River of Our Life*, in which the magical realist had brilliantly argued the need to address the issue of the river's contamination and decay. As far as Ricardo was concerned, one of the worst things to have happened to the Magdalena in modern times was the decision in the 1920s to turn Barranquilla from a river port into a maritime one. Puerto Colombia, the previous port, was abandoned ('with its magnificent pier, the longest in the world, now in fragments'), while Boca de Cenizas had to be made safer by the creation of its line of breakers, 'another ecological disaster'. All the sediment rushing down the Magdalena, he explained, could no longer run freely into the ocean, clogging up the river more than ever.

Alejandro, backed by Juan Alberto, tried getting Ricardo off the subject of catastrophe ('He was never like this before,' he would later confide to me, 'he's becoming a terrible pessimist in his old age'). He announced that he intended taking me the next day to Boca de Cenizas. 'I trust you'll look after him well,' said Ricardo, a wry smile returning to his face as he told me of a sign he had once read on an American boat. 'A collision at sea can ruin your entire day.'

Accidents did happen at Boca de Cenizas. Small boats overturned, people were thrown overboard, and tugs did indeed collide with the ships they were helping into harbour. Alejandro himself had faced death on at least a couple of occasions, he told me as we reached the riverside suburb of Flores, a popular place to come and have lunch. It was now barely breakfast time.

He had spent just a couple of hours in bed before someone from his office had woken him up. Being a pilot, he said, was like being a doctor. When you were on call you were expected to get up even in the middle of the night. A Canadian ship was about to arrive and Alejandro was the one who had to lead it into harbour. We just had time for a coffee in his wooden cabin of an office, where we pored over some nautical charts spread out across the table. Alejandro wanted to show me how much the estuary and coastline had changed over the last century. Whole islands had disappeared, including a well-known local beauty spot, the Isla Verde, which old people remember as having been covered in a mangrove swamp.

We were off. I was greasy with suncream and insect repellent, and trying to prevent a cap bearing the logo of Naviera Fluvial from being blown away by the strong wind. Alejandro had the self-assurance of a yachting champion as he steered our launch at great speed downstream, as if in a race with the waters themselves. We were finally sailing along the Magdalena, passing the last of Barranquilla's houses, skirting a reedy-shored nature reserve controlled until only a few years back by kidnappers.

We approached the fishermen's shacks I had spotted from Gustavo's apartment. A couple of skeletal men in rags walked below a floating row of balloons supporting their fishing hooks. Their homes looked as if they had been washed up on top of a tapering spit of land no more than six metres wide. A single large wave could have put an end to their precarious existence.

The launch bobbed up and down in the river's mouth after the engine was turned off and we boarded an awaiting small tug midstream. We stood on the tug's bridge as we advanced towards the last of the breakers, beyond which was the white-crested sea. Alejandro explained the different instruments on the control panel, emphasizing the total concentration needed for his job. A momentary distraction could be fatal, he said, as the first big swell left my heart in my stomach. I held tightly to a rail as the boat appeared on the point of keeling over before righting itself and rolling the other way. I kept my eyes fixed on the Canadian container vessel ahead, a point of relative stillness in the swaying panorama.

We were only fifty metres away from the ship when the muddy waters we had been following since Flores surged against an expanse of turquoise blue. 'We're there,' shouted out Alejandro, trying to make himself heard against the noise of the engine and the waves. We had reached the undulating line where the waters of the Magdalena joined those of the Caribbean.

Fear turned abruptly to exhilaration, and the rocking boat came to seem like a dancer giving in to unbridled happiness. The union of the waters was a proverbially sexual moment. I remembered a song by the locally born Shakira in which her body yearned to merge into her lover's, 'just as the Magdalena merges into the sea'. Soon I was thinking of other such torrid

Latin songs – songs that sang of ecstasies on moonlit beaches, of beautiful bronzed women with shoulders like maracas, of the spilling of rum and sperm, of the pent-up emotions and memories that find their catharsis in the Caribbean.

But then the tug turned around, and the scene changed. I imagined the first Spaniards nearing the South American mainland at last. They could see enticing sandy beaches backed by palms and the faint silhouettes of impossibly high mountains. Then they saw something else. As they neared the mouth of the river a great mass of murky water rushed towards them. The river seemed so full of energy, so full of the promise of wealth, that they called it 'The Great River'. But its waters were so sinisterly grey that they called its mouth 'The Mouth of Ashes'.

Marcela said she never ate fish from the Magdalena. We were having lunch together at one of Flores' several ramshackle wooden restaurants built on poles over a swampy bank of the river. Thanks to the strong wind and the late Spanish hour the only other clients in the large open-air dining-room were a flirtatious young couple and a group of drunken men at the back. A roof of tattered palms protected us from the sun, but Marcela's thick wavy hair was blowing over her eyes as she explained why she had insisted on ordering food caught in the sea.

'It's nothing to do with pollution,' she said, as we glanced down at eddies of scum and rubbish trapped at the water's edge, 'it's out of respect for the dead. During the worst years of our troubles you could see two or three bodies a day floating down the river.' According to her, a third of the victims of the violence had been disposed of in its waters.

The wind was now blowing so hard that we had to move to a table further from the balcony and then to one further back still. 'We're retreating from the Magdalena,' observed Marcela with a smile. From our more distant and sheltered position the river appeared innocent enough. The agitated tins and plastic bottles were out of sight, and the water looked an attractive russet brown against exotic banks of green. But, as Marcela and I continued talking, the river remained a disconcerting presence in our conversation, a constant reminder of the past, a warning of the future.

'My mother could have told you all about the massacres,' observed Marcela after an uncharacteristically long pause. 'So many of her friends from her village outside Barranquilla were killed. But now that her memory is going, the traumas still remain in some corner of her mind without her being able to recall exactly what they were.'

On the journey from Madrid we had exchanged long stories about our families, and had established a mutual connection with dementia and Alzheimer's. Marcela's mother was still at the conscious stage of memory loss, still able to have told her daughter recently that each time she had a memory she needed to say goodbye to it, for she would never have it again. Losing your memory, she had said, was like staring into an expanding void.

Now Marcela was asking politely after my own mother. She also wanted to hear more about my father. While talking on the plane about our respective backgrounds, I had given a

romanticized version of my parents' meeting in a Sicilian theatre in 1944. I had also spoken about my father's last years,
when he came to dwell almost exclusively on his time as a soldier in Italy.

I had finished reading my father's wartime diaries just
before leaving Europe and they had been much on my mind
ever since. Being in Colombia made it easier for me to imagine the Italy my father had evoked, an Italy whose sensual
beauty, humanity and joy had been balanced by poverty,
despair and the constant nearness of violence and death. The
impact of such a world on my father had been enormous. It
had released him from his middle-class Englishness, increased
his appreciation of life and brought out a latent passionate
nature that would never properly be fulfilled. His diaries, so
much more candid than I had expected, were full of lengthy
passages about his emotional life.

I confessed to Marcela that my father had not directly experienced the horrors of war, as her mother had done. He had
not taken part in any fighting, and had barely seen a corpse.
His job in Intelligence had removed him from the main action,
giving him a great amount of freedom and spare time. His only
duties were to gather political information about the country
and, ironically, to check up on the suitability of marriages
between British soldiers and Italians.

He danced a lot, slept with many women and had his first
piece of writing published in an Italian magazine which
described him as 'one of the greatest exponents of the present
advance guard of the English psychological school'. But there
were times when he admitted being fed up of 'sitting idly on

the margin' of what he considered 'a new period in man's history'.

I kept on thinking about my father even after Marcela moved on to other subjects and started outlining her plans for the Carnival. I was only half-listening to her. The other half of my mind was with my father, trying to imagine him dancing, trying to imagine the women he had been with, the women whose names he must have puzzled over when he came across them again in later life, while rereading his diaries.

There was Betty, his first love, who brought him happiness and heartbreak. There was the older and unconventional Rosalie, who told him he was incapable of loving with true passion. There was the French woman, Josephine, who taught him physical love as no one else had done before. There was Nara, the first of several Italian women who took it for granted he would marry them. And then there was Mafalda, tall, fair-haired and utterly devoted to him, the most enduring of his Italian loves before he met my mother. Mafalda said she would always be waiting for him, no matter how long it took for the war to end and for him to return to Sicily.

'You won't be coming back to Barranquilla,' Marcela declared all of a sudden, waking me from my daydream. 'Something is going to happen to you on the journey. You'll never get to see the Carnival.' I asked her anxiously what she meant by this. She laughed and said she didn't know. 'Perhaps you'll meet the robber of memories,' she teased, holding me by the wrist and telling me we should leave. Flores was not a safe place after dark.

4

'I'm sure I've read something, too, about the robber of memories,' said the driver of the pickup van, as we pondered together the origins of the phrase I had already heard several times in Colombia. I had thought at first it was a line from a García Márquez novel, or else some popular euphemism for Alzheimer's in the more rural parts of the country. But the driver now remembered a folk tale about a robber who came on a horse late at night to steal your memories. When you least expected him.

Then he asked if I had met *el hombre caimán*. 'Now *he* really does exist,' he laughed. 'He lives in the village of Plato, though I don't think he spends his time any more eying naked women bathing in the river. He's a retired mechanic who meets visitors and tourists dressed as a caiman.'

I was heading at last towards the heart of rural Colombia,

towards a land where legend and reality were entwined. Some 'unforeseen problems' had meant that I was doing so for the moment by road. The *Humberto Muñoz*, flagship of the Naviera Fluvial Colombiana, had got stuck on a sandbank while returning from Barrancabermeja to Barranquilla. I was told by Hector Cruz to expect a delay of at least a few days, 'hopefully not more'. This gave me the opportunity to visit earlier than I had planned the once important riverside town of Mompox, on a branch of the Magdalena no longer used by the bigger boats.

The pickup van had collected me from my hotel at four in the morning. Since then I had lost all sense of time and place. Though crammed uncomfortably between the driver and a mother and her young child, I had managed at first to sleep, waking up briefly at dawn to see what I thought was a reddish glint of distant snow. We were passing through yet another village sprawled along the roadside, with its profusion of workshops, bamboo-covered stalls, offerings of fruit juices, coconuts, *arepas*, plantains, pork sandwiches. My eyes were closing again when I caught a sign reading Aracataca, the birthplace of García Márquez, the model for Macondo. Though I might have been dreaming.

The next time I woke up was to hear the driver saying something about a 'donkey library', a *Biblioburro*. Its founder was a teacher from the small village of La Gloria, where we were going to have a breakfast stop long enough for me to see him. He was an 'international celebrity', someone who had to be seen by every traveller passing through the village. At this hour, said the driver, I would find him at his school. The school, a few rows of wooden benches under an awning, was just around the corner from where the van pulled up. The teacher, a smiling, dapper man in his early forties, called his young class to order following the flurry of excitement caused by the arrival of the gringo. He gave them some tasks to do while he went off to talk to me.

We found out immediately that we had a friend in common, Cristian Valencia, the only man in Colombia who made a living writing about his picaresque wanderings around the country. Cristian, a much-loved vagabond on crutches, had begun his literary career after being robbed of all his money during his first and only stay in Europe. As compensation he had insisted that the delinquents who had robbed him tell him the story of their lives. Afterwards, said the teacher, he had come to La Gloria, and encountered the Biblioburro. 'He was the first person to write about me.'

'In the late Nineties,' he continued, 'while teaching young children who had witnessed so many horrors, I became aware more than ever of the beneficial, therapeutic effects of reading. I had this idea for a portable library pulled by donkeys. Then, without any help from the state, I got together about seventy books. Afterwards donations of books came pouring in. The most popular loans are of children's adventure stories. Only one book has ever been stolen from me, a novel by Paulo Coelho that was taken when I was held up by brigands.'

'On leaving the main road at La Gloria, you used to enter a lawless territory under the control of the paramilitaries. Until two or three years ago, an outsider like you would have been stopped immediately,' he said, as he walked with me to the village's outskirts. He wanted to show me his two donkeys, Alfa and Beto, and the small, newly built structure where he housed his library. He then saddled the donkeys, loaded them with books, and mounted Alfa so that I could take his photo.

The van in which I was travelling suddenly appeared, its driver shouting to tell me that we should get going. The teacher urged me to follow the Biblioburro on Facebook, and then searched for a pen to write down his details. Beto, seeing his opportunity to escape from a life of literature, made a wild dash towards a distant patch of green. We ran behind him, joined by one of my fellow passengers, a hitherto silent man whose rural instincts had now joyfully been released. The donkey was scattering books everywhere. I bent down to gather them up, leaving the teacher and the passenger to disappear into a rolling and expanding scrubland dotted with giant trees and palm-thatched adobe huts.

The Mompox road, a badly rutted track, headed slowly down towards the river. I was back inside the van, my head hitting every now and then an exposed bolt in the roof. The passenger who had given chase to the Biblioburro was keeping everyone laughing with tales of sexual initiations involving donkeys. A decrepit old wardrobe we were carrying was groaning alarmingly. The heat outside was rising rapidly, blurring the world around us into a somnolent haze.

A grove of mango trees and a rusting old car ferry were waiting for us at the river's edge. The wardrobe had fallen to pieces, and one of the van's tires had to be repaired while we were being ferried across a narrow stretch of water. The heat was asphyxiating and sweat was stinging my eyes. We landed on a shady island, near a town that had been left to decay. The van left me at a palace in the centre of a Mompox that did not seem at first like a place of bricks, mortar and stone, but rather some memory uncovered from my distant past.

'Mompox does not exist,' says the hero of García Márquez's novel, *The General in his Labyrinth*. 'Sometimes we dream about her, but she does not exist.' The general in question was the Liberator Simón Bolívar, who, having freed South America from Spanish rule, was now a dying man in his late forties, abandoned by most of his friends and supporters, exiled from Bogotá, and on his way to his imminent death in Santa Marta. García Márquez himself admitted that his novel was less a study about illustrious heroes than a eulogy to the Magdalena, the river of the Liberator's final journey.

The Mompox perceived by the disillusioned general on awaking from a delirious fever was a town ruined by years of fighting but still faithful to him, still capable of conjuring up past triumphs and happiness. Though its architecture spoke of the early days of Spanish rule, when it had stored much of Colombia's gold and silver, its recent history was one of enlightened anti-colonialism. It had the oldest university in the Caribbean world and would in 1873 receive as a gift from France a statue of Liberty which preceded that of New York.

But for García Márquez, and for his imagined Bolívar, Mompox was essentially a magical construct of the

Magdalena, a place destined to stagnate, a chronicle in stone of a death foretold. The river that had given birth to the town would eventually be the cause of its terminal decline. The build-up of sediment in the water had reached such a level by the beginning of the last century that river traffic was redirected to the prospering new river-port of Magangué. Mompox, unconnected by bridge to the mainland, became a literal backwater, remote, moribund, barely accessible, guarded by paramilitaries. A place to dream about, a place that might not exist at all.

I thought immediately of the small whitewashed towns of southern Spain, with their palaces of absentee landowners, their streets that came fully alive only towards evening, their blinding whiteness highlighting the blackness of shadows and ironwork grilles. I thought in particular of the town of Osuna, where a horse and cart had once awaited me at the railway station, and nuns from the closed-order convent of the Immaculate Conception had taken care of my washing. But there was something else intensely familiar about Mompox, and I could not think what.

It was midday, and the heat had chased everyone off the streets, and even from the reception area of my chosen hotel, the Doña Manuela, whose rooms were arranged around an enormous arcaded courtyard choked by a tree veined with lianas and exposed roots. A woman eventually came to hand me a key from a wall of keys. I was apparently the only guest. I left my room as soon as I could, to wander around the empty streets in the hope of encountering some form of life. Next to the hotel I peered into the shaded courtyard of another palace,

whose poetic name I later learnt was used in Colombia to sig-
nify a retirement home, *Casa de Recuerdos*, 'House of
Memories'.

I walked down to the river, to a narrow street bordered by
the river's banks and a further row of white, one-storeyed
buildings, sixteenth or seventeenth century in origin, the windows protected by massive grilles, the architectural elements
highlighted in ochre, the plasterwork crumbling and corroded
by damp. A white parapet followed the faint curve of the river,
alongside a row of trees, above banks strewn with what
seemed like a decade's accumulation of rubbish. A worn stone
plinth recorded the various stays in the town of Simón Bolívar,
while above swung the tattered paper streamers of festivities
that were perhaps still waiting to happen. In the far distance
was a brightly painted octagonal church tower said to feature
in a García Márquez novel. I headed towards it.

An old jeep with a broken window, the first car I had seen
since leaving the hotel, was parked alongside the parapet, in front
of an optician's called Optica Marchena. The optician's large
wooden door was open, revealing a dark interior cooled by a
ceiling fan and a tall, slim man slumped on a whicker armchair.
He straightened up as I looked at him. He seemed to be expecting me. He welcomed me in. He had thick black eyebrows, a
deep voice and a smile that exposed prominent teeth. He was
someone I thought I already knew, and I realized why after he
had been talking for a little while, his conversation interrupted
by frequent chuckles, his features contorting when wanting to
give emphasis to a line or to find exactly the right word. He was
almost identical to a close friend of mine from Seville.

Without asking me at first anything about myself, he offered me in turn a chair, a cool glass of the locally made fruit wine, the keys to the car parked outside, a small towel to wipe my profusely sweating brow. He said he always carried such a towel with him whenever he went outside. Mompox was one of the hottest places in Colombia and was now suffering from what he called 'the worst heatwave in years'.

After half an hour of talking I found out that his friends knew him as Nando and that his grandparents had emigrated to Colombia from the Andalucian town of Marchena, between Seville and Osuna. He was not related to my Sevillian friend, but he had a cousin who still ran a Marchena bar I had often frequented.

Nando was an optician who also made money from a small and ailing cattle farm he had inherited. 'There are not enough people in Mompox to make a living purely from prescribing spectacles,' he smiled, getting up to close his shop so that he could come and have lunch with me and show me around the town. He was not expecting more than one or two clients that afternoon, he added, as he went off into a back room to tell his wife that he would be gone for the rest of the day. Equipped now with a towel each, we climbed into the town's only apparent car. 'The pace of life here is different from anywhere I've ever known,' he reflected, after struggling for several minutes with the ignition. 'I was talking earlier today to an elderly neighbour who was sitting outside under a tree. I asked him how he was and what he was up to. He told me he was waiting for a funeral procession to pass.'

*

As we sat at a shaded outdoor table, overlooking the river's rubbish-strewn banks, a friend of Nando's appeared, wearing a baseball cap. He was introduced to me as 'a descendant of the town's original Spanish settlers'. He was like one of the impoverished aristocrats from a Golden Age tale, scrawny and shabby, but with the distinguished, finely sculpted features of an El Greco portrait.

He said he had heard I was in town and he knew of several other people anxiously waiting to meet the 'famous British writer'. He hoped that Nando and I would visit him at his 'palace' later that day. Noticing that the camera I was using was a cheap and malfunctioning one, he also proposed lending me a newly acquired Pentax for my stay in Mompox. Then, as if suddenly remembering some pressing duty, he courteously shook my hand and left. 'The camera is one of his most prized possessions,' commented Nando afterwards, telling me that his friend was officially a dentist, but lived essentially on what was left from his inheritance. 'He spends most of his time researching his family's past. He hasn't even a wife to distract him.'

The heat showed little sign of letting up by late afternoon, when we went to see the fallen aristocrat at his 'palace'. We found him at his dental practice opposite, a cubbyhole stuck in some indeterminate moment of time, with a reclining dentist's chair similar to those of my youth and a general look of having been unused for years. He was typing with one finger at a bulky computer. He said he was doing some genealogical work. He showed me on the screen his family crest and some pages of names dating back to the fifteenth century, among which was that of an ancestor who had been ennobled for his part in the Christian wars against the Moors in Granada.

His ancestral home, entered through an iron-studded wooden door, was a rambling dwelling, with heavy red-leather furniture, various abandoned rooms and walls covered with sepia family portraits. He was telling us about his plans to turn the building into a boutique hotel when a loud knock announced the arrival of a man who referred to himself as 'the poet of Mompox'. 'At last I've caught up with you,' mumbled the poet timidly, his evident emotion competing with his solemn gait and expression.

The poet spoke in a Spanish that was formal and archaic even by Colombian standards. Addressing his town by its full name of Santa Cruz de Mompox, he talked about the 'incomparable honour' of my visiting 'these distant American lands so full of illusions yet so tragically forgotten'. A small article in a Barranquilla newspaper had alerted him to the fact that I might come to Mompox and to my plan of sailing up 'our noble and majestic Magdalena'. He handed me an 'unpublished' poem of his about the Magdalena ('a river that brings up memories') and wrote on it a dedication to his 'dear friend Michael Jacobs, in the hope that this humble work will be of some use to him in his great project'.

The slow peal of funeral bells started sounding and mourners filed past the window grilles of the palace, some carrying the coffin, others shielding themselves with parasols from the relentless sun. After we had all stepped outside to watch them, a burly middle-aged man with a copious moustache pulled up on a motorcycle beside us. He too had been looking for me. He turned out to be the town chronicler, a lawyer and landowner of South Italian origin who wanted us to meet in his house once the funeral mass was over.

By dusk, when our expanding group had reconvened in the chronicler's sitting-room, under a monstrous, slowly rotating ceiling fan, I was pondering again the strange familiarity of Mompox. Three women were embroidering in a dark corner while the men sat around a central table laden with refreshments, devising ways of entertaining me over the coming days. I was in a place I could only have visited before in a dream or in my imagination. Perhaps I was in one of the Sicilian towns my father had described, where he had been treated almost like royalty, introduced to everyone, invited everywhere, encouraged to participate in local intellectual life, flattered into believing that he was a person of importance and brilliance.

The scene in front of me became fleetingly transformed. I was in the town of Syracuse on an April afternoon in 1944. The noise of the ceiling fan became the sound of steady rain, while the grand house I was in had turned into my father's spacious nineteenth-century quarters. My father, exhausted after some heady days of socializing, was with a couple of journalist friends, one of whom was a talented and well-read young writer who came to see him every day. The other person, Franco Libero Belgiorno, was an established magazine editor and drama critic who had brought with him three tickets to a performance that night by a travelling company from Messina. My father would have happily remained where he was, comfortable and dry, and talking about literature. But the forceful

Belgiorno eventually lured him into the rain with the promise of what he said would be a memorable night at the theatre.

Then Nando began talking about iguana eggs. He was determined I should eat some before leaving Mompox. They used to fill the markets, hanging in tresses like garlic, but they were now illegal food and could not be found so easily. To many people, himself included, they were a delicacy that brought back memories of childhood. He would get me some, he promised, as he walked me back late at night to the Doña Manuela. We would have them one day for breakfast.

I would have to wait a while before tasting this Proustian dish, by which time I had got to know another Mompox, a Mompox that was not locked in the past but a town contemplating its transformation into a major tourist centre of the future, an inland Cartagena. A glamorous socialite from Bogotá, engaged in a campaign to clean the river banks of Mompox, took me to see some of her like-minded friends: a brother-in-law of ex-president Uribe, a Spanish banker with a radically modernized palace, and an Austrian craftsman who modelled himself on Gauguin except in his commercial vision and desire to please the local elite. The Austrian cooked us an exquisite supper of fusion cuisine during which he surprised me further with his support of a scheme likely to deprive Mompox of all its romantic atmosphere of remoteness and decay – the construction of a major road bridge. 'Just think,' said the Austrian, 'you'll be able to reach the coast in under two hours. The town will wake up at last to the modern world.'

Nando shared my dismay at this vision. On the morning he finally got hold of some iguana eggs, he recommended I should savour them slowly, 'for one day their flavour might be all that is left to remind us of what Mompox was like'. I took my first bite, into a tiny egg tasting of bitter cod's roe with a texture of sand. I had been expecting an egg that had been laid, an egg with a yolk, not a grainy pouch obtained by slitting open an iguana's stomach. I asked Nando what happens to the rest of the creature. 'We throw it away,' he said. 'No one along the Magdalena eats iguana meat. They only do so in the peninsular of La Guajira.'

'Think of Humboldt,' exhorted Nando a few hours later, after arranging an afternoon excursion on a motorized canoe, 'I'm sure he ate iguana eggs. It's a rite of passage for anyone who travels up the Magdalena.' Our canoe had crossed the river and was cruising along banks swarming with iguanas, who slithered in and out of the water, darting at me what I was convinced were hostile glances. The knowledge that I had condoned their pointless killing weighed on me, and I sensed that this environment I had violated would eventually demand its revenge.

We left the river to drift through the endless lakes and swamps surrounding the town. The winter floods had miraculously spared Mompox, but the livelihood of so many of the people who lived in the nearby hamlets and farms had been destroyed. Whole herds of cattle had been drowned, cultivated fields remained sodden and rotting, and mango trees had withered and gone yellow from too much water.

But the beauty of the world we had entered soon made me

forget almost everything else. A few tiny huts on stilts had precariously survived in a landscape fringed by banks of water lilies, palms and exotic trees in bloom, a landscape in which even the translucent yellows of the dying mangoes had a seductive sensuality. We bathed in waters once ruled by caimans, then stopped off at an enchanted island whose few inhabitants were stewing a turtle for lunch. A parakeet landed on my shoulder, while up above shrieking monkeys jumped from tree to tree.

The darkness came with disconcerting speed. Dramatic clouds, rapidly forming during our final, late-afternoon swim, went suddenly black, then red. The silence was broken by the cries of birds and the buzzing of a million mosquitoes. We headed back as fast as we could. The rain held off, though not the night, which hampered our navigation across shallows, through narrow channels blocked by reeds and overhead branches. A fishing net became entangled in the engine, and for half an hour we were trapped in a world of mysterious sounds, watching the moon rise above the motionless, prehistoric-looking profile of an iguana.

Wednesday was the night when the townspeople of Mompox traditionally congregated at the cemetery. Death in South America is a more public spectacle than it is in Spain, where cemeteries tend to be banished to the ugliest and most remote suburbs. The one at Mompox was situated only a street away from what counted as the centre of local nightlife – a square with a trio of stalls selling drinks and charcoal-grilled meats. On my last night in town, a Wednesday night, I relaxed on the square with Nando, planning to go on afterwards to one of the weekly gatherings at the tombs.

I had been in Mompox far longer than I had anticipated. Nando reminded me that travellers in the past had never been able to predict how long they would be staying there. In the days before steam travel, they had been at the mercy of the boatmen known as *bogas*, who, on reaching Mompox – the home town of so many of them – got perpetually drunk and kept on postponing their departure. I was at the mercy, instead, of the Naviera Fluvial. The *Humberto Muñoz* was still grounded somewhere north of Barrancabermeja, and for a while I had almost given up on the idea of journeying up the river on a big vessel. But then Hector Cruz rang to say that alternative arrangements had been made. I needed to get back to Barranquilla as soon as possible.

News of my departure from Mompox spread as quickly as the news of my arrival. Members of Nando's circle – the poet, the chronicler, the fallen aristocrat – soon joined us for a bottle of rum on the square. They wanted to say goodbye. They also did not want me to miss the Wednesday *tertulia* at the cemetery, a ritual claimed by the chronicler to be unique to Colombia.

Even though the rum made us light-headed, the conversation in the square revolved almost exclusively around cemeteries. Nando told us a 'true story' about a small Amazonian river-port whose inhabitants were forbidden to die until a cemetery was built. 'And no one did die until the local cemetery was finally completed, after which everyone started dying.' The poet followed this with a mention of the cemetery at Puerto Berrío, a port I would actually be passing if I 'managed to make it south of Barrancabermeja'. The place, he said, was where the families of those who 'disappeared' during the troubles annually invoked the spirits of the dead to help them recover their loved ones.

As we walked at last towards the cemetery, shortly before midnight, I recalled a large map of Colombia that hung in a back room of Nando's practice. It was covered with tiny flags that marked the places where people had been kidnapped or 'disappeared' at the hands of guerrillas and paramilitaries. An especially large cluster covered the upper reaches of the Magdalena. Nando told me that the flags were his way of ensuring that the victims were never forgotten.

I was still picturing the map and the exact location of the flags as we approached the dimly lit cemetery, where I could vaguely make out hushed groups of people behind an open ironwork gate. To the faint but inappropriate accompaniment of a carnival band playing in an adjoining street, the poet read out the inscription placed above the cemetery's entrance. 'This is the frontier that separates life from death,' he recited in the portentous voice of a ham actor. I was trying to suppress my laughter until a brief and unaccountable shudder went through me. The background music had stopped for a few seconds and all I could hear were the murmurings of the cemetery's nocturnal visitors. I felt as if I were truly nearing the land of the dead.

PART TWO
UPRIVER

5

'I remember everything about the river, absolutely everything.'
The words of the old writer resurfaced in my mind as the hour
for embarking finally arrived. Like the words of the opening of
a tale, they led me back into the past, to the moment when the
writer, as a fifteen-year-old boy, leaving home for the first time,
was taken by his family to the port at Barranquilla. It was
January 1943, the very month and year of my father's departure for Sicily, over a quarter of a century before my parents
dropped me at London's Victoria Station, at the start of a journey to Spain that would consolidate my love of the Hispanic
world and of travelling. I had enrolled as a language student
in the southern Spanish town of Córdoba. I too had been fifteen, and had never been away before on my own. My mother
had made me a crude money bag out of one of my vests, and
prepared a day's supply of tuna-and-egg sandwiches. One of

her more lasting memories was of sensing my anxiety as she and my father waved goodbye as the train pulled away. She did not sleep properly that night, nor would she for several nights to come. She wondered if she would ever see me again.

The voice of Hector Cruz, cheerier and more positive than I had ever heard it, brought me back to the present and to the private yacht club at the head of a narrow, secretive inlet hemmed in by palms and dense vegetation. I was sipping from a chilled glass of beer as I heard him tell me that the tugboat I would soon be boarding was not quite as comfortable as the *Humberto Muñoz*, but would be carrying the heaviest cargo ever transported in Colombia – two giant cylindrical tanks intended for the petrol refinery at Barrancabermeja. Hector, as excited as a schoolboy on an outing, had taken the morning off from the office to see me on my way and witness what he called 'an historic moment in Colombia's history'.

An uncommunicative photographer, with a shaven head and a designer goatee beard, had been brought along to record the day's momentous events. The other person sitting with us in the club's open, bamboo-covered bar was a friend of mine from Bogotá, Julio Caycedo, who had offered to accompany me all the way to the Magdalena's source. Reluctantly I had come round to accepting Hector's advice that I would be much safer travelling with a Colombian than on my own. Many other people had also said that a solitary gringo would be especially vulnerable where I was going.

I discreetly watched Julio as he tried to show interest in what Hector was telling us by taking out a notebook and recording that each of the tanks coming with us upriver was sixty-three metres long by seven metres wide, and weighed 640 tons. 'That makes a total tonnage of 1,280!' announced Hector, perhaps expecting astonished gasps from his audience. Julio nodded and continued writing, his narrow and distinguished face remaining impassive, his expression hidden behind a pair of dark glasses. Later, after Hector had stood up to look for the waiter, I detected a slight smile beneath several days of stubble. He was returning my glance. I could tell that his first impressions of Hector were the same as mine had been.

I barely knew Julio, but I had had an intuition he would be the perfect person to travel with around Colombia. We had met the year before in Bogotá, where his wife had organized literary activities coinciding with the bicentenary celebrations. I had spent an evening with the two of them, getting away from officialdom, hearing alternative views about Colombia's presidency, visiting lively student haunts and discovering a mutual taste in popular dives and eateries. I had not seen him again until last night, a few hours after he had flown in from Bogotá. A combination of his sudden immersion in the Caribbean world, and an afternoon of drinking rum with an old school friend, had filled him with an excess of emotion and energy. He was asking every woman in the street if they would dance with him.

I was rapidly finding out more and more about Julio, not least his ability to adapt to every type of social situation. The uninhibited hedonist of the night before had become by morning the fundamentally serious and reliable person I had perceived on our first encounter. Though his shorts and sleeve-less vest had drawn disapproving looks at Hector's office, he was soon winning people over with his charm and exquisite courtesy. On being asked for some personal information for the Naviera Fluvial's records, he seemed to have impressed Hector by revealing that his father's surname was the grand-sounding Ponce de León (the name of one of the great military heroes of fifteenth-century Spain) and that he was a journal-ist. Later, in private, he would tell me that he far preferred to use his more ordinary, maternal surname of Caycedo. As for his work as a journalist, of which I had had no idea, he said that he had a press card which he had left at home, 'just in case we have some unwanted encounters on our journey'. Guerrillas and paramilitaries were understandably suspicious of anyone who appeared to be investigating their activities.

A launch was waiting at the yacht club to take us to our boat, but Hector announced that we had plenty of time to spare, and ordered another round of drinks. This gave him the opportunity to tell us more about the Naviera Fluvial, all of whose boats were named after some aspect of Humberto Muñoz's life. Four of them bore the names of his dead chil-dren. I learnt that none of these children had died while travelling along the Magdalena, as Humberto's memoir had unwittingly suggested. One had mysteriously fallen from a bal-cony, another had been killed in a car crash and a third after falling off a motorcycle. A fourth child, Catalina, had been one of the victims of the 'El Nogal atrocity of 2003'.

Afterwards, when we had been provided with life jackets and were finally walking down the pier to the waiting launch,

Julio explained to me that El Nogal was an exclusive Bogotá club whose bombing by FARC guerillas in 2003 had significantly changed attitudes towards Colombia's civil conflict. The country's wealthy elite had hitherto thought of this conflict as something primarily affecting poor people in remote rural areas. But the violence had now reached the privileged enclaves of Colombia's capital. From that moment on, no one felt safe.

I interrupted Julio in mid-sentence. My cellphone was ringing. The line was faint and halting, but I could just about hear my mother's Filipino carer talking to me. She seemed to be saying that my mother had been taken ill and was now in hospital, and that she was desperately asking for me. Then the line went dead. I tried ringing back but the signal had gone. I did not know what to do. I followed the others and stepped onto the launch.

The launch sped down the hidden inlet, past banks of herons and into the epic expanse of the Magdalena, with its views of Barranquilla's faraway tower blocks, and of a row of ships, containers and cranes lined up in front of the faintly visible Pumarejo Bridge. I could barely concentrate on the surroundings. I had woken up at dawn with a premonition of imminent drama. Now I had a vision of my mother dying far from her two sons. I imagined my brother uncontactable at some important meeting in Dublin, Brussels or Strasbourg, while I was frantically trying to get back from Colombia.

Without a phone signal there was no way of my judging the seriousness of her condition. And, if I were going to have to

return to England, I would have to decide this almost immediately, before reaching the tugboat to which we were rapidly
heading. Once I had boarded I anticipated being trapped there
for days, cut off from the world at large, stuck perhaps on a
sandbank.

Finally, the phone rang again. The voice at the other end
was just about audible over the roar of the launch's engine. A
hospital nurse was speaking. 'She's as fit as a fiddle, your
mum ... Aren't you, my dear?' Then my mother spoke, in a
voice that gave no hint that anything was wrong with her. She
asked me how I was, and said that she herself was fine and was
visiting a few friends. When I told her I was in Colombia, she
hoped I was enjoying my holiday.

Our launch was now gliding the remaining metres to what
looked like a streamlined version of the *David Arango*, the
passenger boat compared by Isherwood to a Mississippi
steamer 'in the days of Mark Twain'. Only the steam paddle
was missing. The vessel, resembling a flattened wedding cake
striped with the bright blues, reds and yellows of the
Colombian flag, had three decks, the upper one supporting a
bridge with a pagoda-like hat, the lowest one almost touching the water. Four sailors were attaching to the bow a barge
carrying the two giant tanks whose exact tonnage I had
already forgotten, but whose size more than doubled that of
our boat. I could not see how we were going to push such
monsters.

I was beginning to turn my mind again to matters other
than my mother, to feel once more the mounting thrill of a
major journey on the point of being realized after so much

anticipation, so many delays. But the sense of something sinister, floating just beneath the surface, and waiting to emerge, had not entirely gone away. I found it disquieting that our boat was called the *Catalina*, after a woman killed by terrorists.

Hector took us straight away to meet the captain, an Afro-Colombian who looked like a jovial, overweight blues singer past his prime. He wobbled and wheezed as he walked, his hair was peppered white and a massive silver chain glinted beneath his capacious green overalls. As he opened his mouth to talk, his eyes almost disappeared beneath the fat of his cheeks, as if he were about to break into a soulful song. He lifted his hand to slap it down hard into mine and then Julio's. He had an open face, a deep laugh and a voice that quivered and went shrill in moments of excitement. He told us that his was a name we would never forget, Diomidio Raimundo Rosales. Then he roared again with laughter.

We chatted briefly under the ultramarine awning of the boat's gangway, where we were introduced to the boat's other 'voice of authority', Alfredo. Alfredo told us that he was the person in charge of the two tanks, and that he and Diomidio had worked together for over twenty years and he knew no one else with so many stories to tell about the Magdalena. They made an odd pair. Alfredo stood out as the only member of the crew who was neither of obvious African descent, nor a *zambo* (someone with that admixture of African and Indian blood which predominated along the Magdalena). Instead he had an almost Central European look, with pasty, greasy skin and an overall seriousness that contradicted his early attempt to win me onto his side by asking with an insinuating grin what I thought of Colombia's women. He appeared anxious to be liked, yet remained introverted, troubled, unlovable.

It seemed that Diomidio and Alfredo were to be our main companions on the journey, the two people with whom we would be sharing all our meals and who occupied the other two cabins of the privileged central deck. Our future living quarters, enclosed on either side by stiff metal and glass doors, hummed continuously with the combined noises of the engine, a rattling and over-efficient air-conditioning system and the poorly amplified sounds of a television. The latter, attached to a bracket, projected over an uninviting area comprising a Formica dining table, a tiny hand basin and a scattering of plastic chairs. Diomidio's office was at the opposite end of the deck to this 'recreational zone'. It was dominated by a large computer which Diomidio described as working only sporadically and with the speed of a 'carrier pigeon'. He said I was free to use it for my 'own private purposes'. He gave me a wink.

The cabin earmarked for me and Julio was inbetween Diomidio's and Alfredo's. But Hector told us that it was not yet ready for us and a problem had occurred that was 'currently being resolved'. Then he went off with the two commanders to attend to the final preparations before the boat was ready to sail.

Julio and I decided to go on an exploratory tour of the rest of the boat, equipped with the life jackets that Diomidio had pronounced obligatory whenever we went outdoors. We descended to the lower deck, where most of the sailors had their cabins, alongside the smells of the galley and the violent rumbling of the boat's exposed machinery. The heat and the pounding of the engine soon made us climb back upstairs, to make our way to the bridge. A cook intercepted us halfway, carrying a tray of food. Our lunch was on the point of being served. Hector and our two new friends were waiting for us at the Formica table. Alfredo crossed himself when the food arrived.

Hector appeared to regard Diomidio in the same larger-than-life light that Alfredo did, but in a somewhat patronizing way. Diomidio for him was the archetypal river captain, a near-fictional figure who had seen and done every-thing in his forty-five years of navigating the Magdalena and whose main purpose now in life was to entertain people with his tales. Diomidio lived up to this reputation by telling us about his encounter many years back with the 'strange mammal that few other people have been lucky enough to see on the river'.

With his eyes reduced to slits and his hands fully extended in the air, Diomidio prefaced his story by recollecting the time when the Magdalena swarmed with wild life and caimans 'eagerly awaited sailors who fell overboard'. But what he saw 'fifteen years ago, almost to this very day' was something he would never forget. 'I've seen many bizarre, marvellous and horrific sights on this river but I'll always remember that February afternoon in 1996 when a massive creature with webbed feet, a duck-bill and a tail like that of a beaver crawled out of the water and lay on the bank.'

I tried to imagine what animal this could possibly be, but Diomidio could only vaguely remember its name. 'Someone said it was an *Ornitodólogo* or an *Ornitinko*. It was certainly an Orni-something-or-other. I was told it had a spur on its foot that delivered a deadly poison.'

'An *ornitorrinco*?' suggested Julio, naming an animal I assumed was from a mythical bestiary, until I realized this was the Spanish name for a duck-billed platypus. My knowledge of natural history was sufficient to know that the platypus was an Australian animal unheard of in South America. 'Yes, that was it, an *ornitorrinco*, an *ornitorrinco*!' shouted the excited Diomidio.

Julio and I later speculated as to whether the platypus had escaped from the drug baron Pablo Escobar's private zoo, whose liberated hippos were still said to be wallowing in mud-flats further up the river. More likely, the sighting of the animal was a pure invention on Diomidio's part or else a delusion brought on by too many years of going up and down the river. Or perhaps the explanation had something to do with the world into which we were heading, a world I envisaged as existing on the boundaries of reason.

We were on the bridge when the *Catalina* and its record-breaking cargo finally set sail. Hector was still with us, waiting for the moment when the boat passed under the low arches of the Pumarejo Bridge, whose short-sighted construction in 1974 had been another tragedy in the Magdalena's history. The photographer was stationed on the launch, already getting into position to take the perfect shot of a sight that might once have appeared indicative of modernity, commercial confidence and faith in the future – the arrival at the concrete bridge of two massive cylindrical tanks festooned with the banners of the 'NAVIERA FLUVIAL COLOMBIANA'.

Diomidio was retelling his story of the platypus to a couple of his crew. One of them, a pensive young pilot whom everyone referred to by his full name Juan Cano, was at the helm, trying to give his full attention to the problem of steering the boat towards the bridge while the view in front of him was blocked by the two parallel tanks. His face wore the slight, bored smile of someone who had heard Diomidio's stories hundreds of times before and no longer found them at all remarkable. His colleague, a plump man with prominent braces and the face of someone who liked telling jokes and making fun of everything, sniggered at the conclusion of the tale, and then offered to get me a cup of coffee. He wondered if this act of kindness would earn him a place 'in your next book'.

There was still some way to go before reaching the bridge. I reckoned that at our current rate of travel, little faster than if we had been jogging, we had a good five minutes left. Hector, pausing from taking calls and photos on his cellphone, made use of the time by telling us about piloting a riverboat. He surprised me by saying that people such as Juan Cano and his jester colleague with the braces received no official training for the job. Unlike the man who had taken me to Boca de Cenizas, they did not have to attend years at a piloting school, but were simply ordinary sailors who had shown a particular aptitude for a job that Hector described as 'more demanding than any other, given the unpredictability of the Magdalena'.

'For a start,' he stressed, 'you need a remarkable memory. You need to know each curve, each tiny variation in the river. You need to remember the position of each hidden obstacle, the parts of the river likely to create problems ...' As we were talking, the boat suddenly stopped. I worried about our future progress if we were experiencing problems less than twenty minutes after we had started. But Juan Cano pointed to a distant launch that was coming in our direction. We were waiting for it to catch up with us.

Hector carried on. He said that when he had started working with the company, the pilots did not even have the benefit of a good radar, or any instrument to test the depth of the water. 'Now, of course, the Naviera Fluvial has equipped its boats with the most up-to-date technology. Though this took some persuading on my part.'

The launch had now arrived. A complex and lengthy series of manoeuvres ensued, involving much shouting and the rushing around of half a dozen sailors. Only after a while did Julio and I realize what they were doing, and why our cabin had not been ready for us. Someone had forgotten to furnish it. History had been delayed while someone had gone to buy sheets, mattresses and the frame of a bunk bed, all of which were now being loaded on board.

We resumed our course towards the bridge. The photographer repositioned himself. Everyone went briefly silent as the tanks slid underneath the concrete beams. Julio whispered to me that he thought the cargo would not make it. He judged that it had got through with barely half a metre to spare. 'But I assume that someone had carefully calculated the measure-

ments beforehand,' he commented light-heartedly. We would
soon learn not to assume anything.

Hector and the photographer left us soon afterwards. The
atmosphere on the boat noticeably started to change. The rule
about life jackets was relaxed, and Julio and I happily dis-
pensed with them as we brought out two chairs to sit on the
gangway, to watch the unfolding of a grand spectacle whose
every detail we thought at first worthy of writing down in our
identical Moleskine notebooks.

Seeing the Pumarejo Bridge and the last of Barranquilla's
buildings vanish behind us heightened the liberating sensation
of having properly embarked on a journey into the unknown.
The river seemed progressively more immense. The distant
wooded banks were becoming ever further apart, as if the flow
of water against us was an illusion and we were not going
upriver at all, but downriver, towards an ocean.

I was so enveloped by the Magdalena's grandeur that I did
not immediately register the presence of the cook beside me.
He had come to tell us that supper was ready. It was 4.30 in
the afternoon and we had only recently finished lunch. The
cook explained that it had been an unusual day today, but we
were now back to what he said was the boat's normal eating
schedule.

Diomidio greeted us like long-lost friends, and Alfredo was
already crossing himself prior to tucking in to a meal that
looked almost the same as the one we had had two hours earlier. We sat down in front of them, feeling disappointed at
having had our enjoyment of the river abruptly curtailed, and

wondering if we could manage a plate piled up with fish, rice and leathery fried plantains. Diomidio's and Alfredo's appetites were clearly unaffected, with Alfredo attacking the fish as if determined not to miss out on the tiniest morsel. He sucked dry every single bone, cleaning up the fish more thoroughly than I've ever seen anyone do before. For Julio, this was confirmation of the man's 'anally retentive personality'.

Diomidio, without Hector in the room, was able to speak to us with complete openness. He said how much he had come to hate his job, and how he had only 'two months and twelve days left before retiring'. He was counting the days. He could barely wait for them to be over. He was badly paid, and managed on average to be at home for only thirty-two days of the year. He now had two grandchildren and wanted to spend more time with them. Two of his own children had been fortunate enough to have had a university education. 'I wouldn't wish my own life on anyone.'

Navigation along the Magdalena used to be 'beautiful', he added. But then everything changed. The river's problems mounted, and there was a surge in 'hooliganism and delinquency'. A turning point for him seemed to have been the death on the river of one of his best friends, 'perhaps the greatest pilot the Magdalena has ever known'. The death of this person, he admitted, was a purely accidental one, but it had reinforced his morbid feelings towards the river. His friend had died after slipping off the *Catalina*. His head had hit a wooden spike. His body had swollen up terribly after the intake of so much water. 'It had to be cut up to be carried.'

Other tales of death soon followed, with the conversation

touching on the period in the Nineties when the Magdalena
had turned into a metaphorical river of blood. 'Since then
we've always carried soldiers,' said Diomidio, announcing that
eight of them would be joining us tomorrow, 'expanding our
numbers to around twenty-four'.

I had forgotten to mention the soldiers to Julio and, having
not seen any board at Barranquilla, had imagined they would
not be coming with us after all. Julio did not like the idea of
the soldiers. Though he did not express his misgivings to
Diomidio, he thought their presence would turn us 'into a
moving target'.

'Today of course they're just a standard security measure,'
reassured Diomidio, trying to make light of the whole matter.
'It's been years since we've been attacked, and we've never had
a kidnapping or a killing.'

Julio and I returned to our seats on the gangway, each of us
secretly working out what we would do when we came under
a hail of bullets from the river's banks. We heard more about
earlier attacks from one of the many sailors who stopped to
talk to us as he passed by. Tall, muscular and with jet-black
skin, he had emerged solemn-faced from the infernally loud
and hot engine room. He said he had experienced six attacks
while working as an engineer on the *Catalina*. Each of them
had seemed scarier than the last, though he knew of only one
boat, belonging to a rival company, whose cargo had been successfully seized. 'The sailor on watch duty that night had fallen
asleep.'

The engineer offered to show us the bullet holes. The boat
had been thoroughly refurbished since the 1990s, with the

railings of the gangways replaced by bullet-proof balustrades with gun emplacements so that the soldiers on board could fire back. But the marks of bullets could still be seen all over the steel bulwark if you knew where to look for them. The engineer remembered the position of every one. They were permanent reminders for him of the mortal risks of the Magdalena journey.

We sailed slowly in the softening light through what had been the antechamber of hell. I was once again imagining the past. It was April 1536, and the 800-strong troops of the Spanish conquistador Jiménez de Quesada were setting off on the largest inland expedition ever mounted from the coastal town of Santa Marta. Half of them were travelling by ship to the Magdalena, and the others by horse and on foot, with the aim of joining up at the end of a stretch of river first explored seven years earlier by the Portuguese sailor Jerónimo de Melo. The strange colour and unusual strength of the waters at Boca de Cenizas should have served as a warning. So should the story of Melo's expedition, which had been under almost constant attack from arrows fired by hostile Indians from the banks and from canoes.

The sufferings of Quesada's troops would be even worse. The fragile river boats were initially prevented by a storm from entering the Magdalena, with one of them being smashed to pieces and its survivors ending up in the hands and mouths of a cannibal tribe. Greatly delayed and reduced in numbers, the river troops had eventually met up with the overland ones only to find that the latter had fared no less disastrously. The reunited forces exchanged the most appalling tales of misery: of tropical diseases, of the relentless heat and humidity, of fatal snake bites, of intestinal worms that grew to enormous size, of savage attacks by jaguars and caimans, of poisoned arrows that made their victims die mad and in agony, of a plague of insects that caused such perpetual moaning that Quesada was obliged to command his men to silence.

Still they persevered, the weakest soldiers by boat, the others by jungle tracks barely passable in the rainy season. Driven on by an exaggerated intuition that Spain would 'get greater service from the Magdalena than from all the Indies together', they envisaged gold at the end of the river, or at least a shortcut to Peru. Their maniacal efforts would eventually be rewarded, though not as they had originally thought, and only after being defeated by cataracts beyond the present-day town of Honda. Leaving the valley to climb into the Andes, they encountered the emerald-rich kingdom of the Muiscas, and founded in August 1538 the future Colombian capital of Santa Fe de Bogotá.

All later travellers approaching Bogotá from the coast had no choice but to do what Quesada's men had done: to sail up the Magdalena as far as Honda. They braved the attacks of Indians for a further hundred years. They endured the other dangers and hardships of the journey right up to the age of the steamship. Their means of transport remained for centuries the indigenous *champán*, a covered barge rowed by teams of overworked and often inebriated boatmen. The painfully slow progress upstream involved the additional use of poles. The strong currents in the centre of the river made the boats regularly capsize. But navigating close to the banks meant risking the poisonous snakes that dangled from the low overhead branches. Insects devoured the passengers at dusk. Dangerous animals savaged them on sandbanks at night. Electrical storms created daily spectacles of terrifying magnitude. Exhaustion, illness and despair finished off even the strongest constitutions.

Blair Niles, a restless American traveller of the early twentieth century, described – in her book *Colombia: Land of Miracles* (1924) – a journey upriver in the company of passengers who talked about 'the Magdalena of their grandfathers, when people contemplating a trip on this difficult river made their wills and paid possibly final farewells to family and friends'. From the luxury of her boat, those days of precarious travel must have seemed unlikely to recur. She could not have predicted the fear provoked later in the twentieth century by guerrillas and paramilitaries. She could not have envisaged the Magdalena turning once again into one of the world's most dangerous thoroughfares.

We rose from our chairs on the gangway, sprayed ourselves with insect repellent and donned our life jackets once more. With Diomidio shouting out behind us to be careful, we climbed down to the lower deck, and started making our slow and cautious way to the tip of the barge carrying the two tanks.

The water was almost at our feet as we nimbly negotiated the narrow passage between the river and the side of one of the tanks, on which was painted some words I had not noticed before: 'Extreme Danger, Cargo Containing Nitrogen.' Were we really transporting a potentially massive bomb needing only a single bullet to ignite? 'Who knows,' shrugged Julio, once we had reached the empty stretch of platform at the bow. We had gone there to watch the day ending.

A couple of sailors had got there before us. They were setting up a wooden tripod to which they were going to attach a simple lantern. There was no other lighting on the barge, no other way of signalling at night our possibly explosive cargo.

My cellphone rang just as we came to the outskirts of a village. I answered nervously, but the news was good. A doctor had found nothing wrong with my mother, who would be allowed home early the next day. I felt a sense of calm as I took in the arrival of dusk and the gathering mystery of the surroundings.

We were cruising near a wooded bank, moving towards the red dome of a parish church. I asked one of the sailors the name of the village. He replied as if responding to a memory test, giving me not only the village's name but also its exact distance in kilometres from Barranquilla. His answer testified to the slowness of our progress. 'Remolino, *kilómetro* 34.5.'

The large and untidy church square led down to the river via a broad flight of worn steps. The church had a white and ochre facade crowned with consoles and volutes. A group of children was playing on the square. A boy was flying a purple kite. The village was disappearing into a darkening bank of trees. Yellowing mango leaves glimmered in the sylvan obscurity. A couple of horses were being washed at the water's edge. A fisherman in a dugout canoe hurried past. A camp fire was blazing in the threshold of an isolated hut.

I thought of my mother and how her visual perception of the world around her had become more acute than ever as dementia had taken hold of her. She always used to say to me that she valued sight more than any other of her faculties. She said she would far rather be deaf and dumb than blind. She probably would have preferred losing her mind as well, if she had ever considered that a possibility.

Her sight was now her principal support. She could no longer reason, could barely hear and was even losing her sense of taste and smell. But little escaped her eyes. Seeing was her life's main remaining pleasure, perhaps her only pleasure. She loved the flowers I always gave her and observed each little change in them in a way few others would. Though her state of mind made her unable to distinguish, say, between the flowers themselves and an effect of light on the window behind them, she would notice such details as the hourly appearance of each leaf, the emergence of the tiniest new buds, the minutest details of decay. 'At least I have my flowers,' she would say in moments of emotional upset.

I could sense how much she would have enjoyed being where I was now, scanning the trees on the banks, detecting their blossom in the twilight, fussing about the colour of the mangoes, wondering what the fire was for, beaming like a little girl at the sight of the first red streaks in the evening sky.

We saw the sunset from the end of the barge, facing a horizon of reddish-brown water, seated on bollards like a couple of figures from a Romantic canvas contemplating infinity. The return of the sailors back to the tugboat had left us here on our own, absorbing, for the first time since Barranquilla, what almost amounted to silence. The noise of the boat's engine was now a distant rumble muffled by the gentler sound of moving water. The wooded banks around Remolino, with their cries of children and birds, were becoming a faint black line as we veered towards the centre of a river that seemed to be broadening all the time.

An abrupt jolt disturbed our dreaming. A sandbank, guessed Julio as the boat remained worryingly still for what seemed like ages, before retreating backwards in fits and starts. Finally, after a slight change of course, we were again aiming upstream and appearing to progress smoothly. Julio judged this a good moment to make 'our offering to the river'.

He explained that he had once travelled along an Amazonian tributary of the Magdalena. He had met some Indians there who had assured him that the water from the river was perfectly safe to drink, but only after you had taken and spat out three handfuls of it and asked the river's permission. He had done as he was told, and was not sick once. The Indians had also taught him about the importance of the offering.

He took some tobacco from a pouch and gave me some as well. We then got to our feet, went to the edge of the barge and threw the tobacco into the water in front of us. We hoped the river would remember this gesture as our boat headed ever deeper into the dark emptiness.

6

'Cerro San Antonio, *kilómetro* 82,' murmured the pilot Juan Cano as he passed me on the gangway at the end of his night shift. It was just after five in the morning, and I had got up early to watch the day begin. I was looking towards a handful of lights under the still-dark sky.

Clear conditions had allowed us to sail throughout the night. We were probably little more than an hour's drive away from Barranquilla, but there was no point in thinking in those terms. We had moved into another sphere of existence in which hours, days and weeks had a different meaning than they had had before, and where life was regulated by the names of obscure places and their distances in kilometres that were not real kilometres, but numbers to be memorized for no apparent purpose.

Juan Cano paused for a few moments beside me, as if wanting to tell me something else, something of real importance. But he smiled and went away, leaving me to the darkness and the sound of an engine that had become like a perpetual tinnitus. I sat down next to the bullet-proof balustrade, waiting for the day.

A shrill voice disturbed the pre-dawn stillness. My name was being called, my diminutive name in Spanish, the familiar name normally used only by my most intimate friends, but appropriated now in distorted fashion by Captain Diomidio Raimundo Rosales. '*Migueleeeto!*' he cried, as I turned around to receive the slap of his hand against mine. He told me about the wonderful progress we had made during the night, and that we would be reaching the town of Calamar, our first official stop, by 'around nine in the morning, way before schedule'.

I went indoors for a six o'clock breakfast, which was confusingly almost the same as what we had had for lunch and supper, but with slabs of indeterminate, gravy-coloured meat. The cook, on removing my plate, said that lunch would be at ten. Through the porthole I could faintly glimpse another village, profiled against the first grey streaks of dawn.

'Charanga, *kilómetro* 85.7,' intoned Diomidio. I could have been listening to the ticking of a clock.

I had gone to bed under a starlit sky, but the dawn was heavy and dull. A sailor with a bucket had just washed down the bow deck, where I found Alfredo standing with Julio, talking about the floods. We were travelling through the part of the Magdalena Valley most affected by them, nearing the point where the river is joined by the canal that unites it with the sea at Cartagena, the Canal del Dique. The Spaniards built the canal in the late sixteenth century so that ships could avoid entering the Magdalena through the ill-famed Boca de Cenizas. On 30 November 2010 this regularly reconstructed waterway burst its banks, obliterating whole communities and reducing others such as Charanga to just a few standing houses. The area's inhabitants were only now beginning to return to their villages, but thousands remained homeless, put up in camps, schools and the houses of well-wishers.

'I prefer not to think about the exact number of people who were killed or left with nothing,' sighed Alfredo. 'It's too painful.' Like all the Colombians with whom I had spoken about the floods, Alfredo blamed the government for its failure to take preventive measures. He told us mournfully about the state-run Magdalena Company, which had been formed in 1991 to control the river and the Canal del Dique. 'They have been utterly useless.'

Diomidio, stepping out onto the deck, overheard what Alfredo was saying. 'You can always rely on Alfredo to tell the truth,' he commented in a half-jocular tone, before becoming deadly serious himself. He declared that the 'great curse of Colombia is its politicians'.

'The politicians in Bogotá haven't paid the slightest attention to the Magdalena Company,' he continued, his voice rising with emotion. 'Any time someone has anything sensible to suggest they always turn it down. A hydraulic engineer from Holland proposed a brilliant solution that had already been pioneered in his own country. He offered to line the

Magdalena's banks with walls that could be lowered during the summer months, and raised again in time for the winter rains. But the politicians rejected him. They couldn't care a damn about the river. If they wanted to they could turn it again into what it always was – one of this continent's great commercial thoroughfares. You know, it's far cheaper and more ecological to transport goods by river than by road. But it's not in the politicians' interests to do so, just as it wasn't in their interests to maintain a rail service in this country. And shall I tell you why? Because all the senators have their money invested in roads.'

Diomidio paused to allow Julio to explain to me that all the main roads in Colombia were privately owned, and that the money from the many toll booths mostly benefited politicians. 'But I shouldn't have brought up the subject,' interrupted Diomidio. 'If I were to speak in Barrancabermeja as I've just spoken to you now a hired assassin on a motorcycle would probably finish me off.' He gave out one of his booming laughs.

We were already arriving at Calamar, even earlier than Diomidio had estimated. It was just after seven. The first of a line of multicoloured riverside houses was visible behind a water tank said by Alfredo to have belonged to a now-vanished railway station. In front of this was the opening of the Canal del Dique, from which appeared an ageing, grey tug-boat. Canoes and a *chalupa* scurried past us as we moored against a floating platform a hundred metres from the canal. The sky was streaked by flights of birds. The sun was burning through the clouds.

*

We would be stopping at Calamar for the time it took to attach four more barges to our already lengthy cargo. Julio and I wanted to visit the town. Though we had barely spent nineteen hours on the boat, we were beginning to feel increasingly cocooned from the outside world. Our life on board, with all its constrictions and idiosyncrasies, had become the new normality. We needed a break.

The day before, when Hector had still been with us, we had asked if we would have the opportunity to look around Calamar, an obligatory port of call in the days of the steamship. Hector, seconded by Diomidio, had discouraged us from going there, saying that I would stick out like a sore thumb and the place was dangerous for any outsider.

Diomidio, now only too delighted to grant us shore leave, phoned a boatman he knew to pick us up and accompany us on our visit. Alfredo made insinuating comments about the openness of the Calamar women. The pilot with the braces giggled and gave us the thumbs-up sign.

'Take your time, don't rush things!' laughed Diomidio as we boarded a rickety wooden boat ferrying a couple of women to the market. An outboard motor was turned on and the boat pulled away from the *Catalina* with a speed that seemed like that of an aeroplane taking off. We were aiming towards a polychromatic shoreline crowded with strolling people, bicycles and rickshaws.

Isaac Holton, a footloose American travelling up the Magdalena in the 1850s, described Calamar as a 'dull, mean village ... on a flat plain, with uninteresting vegetation'. Six years later a visitor from Bogotá, José María Samper, spoke of

Calamar as a place with 'a great agricultural and commercial future' and inhabitants who were 'friendly and expansive'. My own impression, on drawing up at a steep bank lined with bobbing rows of pirogues, was that I had arrived in Africa.

The scene was eerily reminiscent of the Niger river-port of Mopti, which I had got to know many years back, on my way to Timbuktu. Julio, with his broad-rimmed olive-green canvas hat, looked like a young European explorer on his way to recruit bearers for an expedition into the interior. Numerous potential recruits were waiting for us on top of the bank, but the boatman waved them away. He had proudly assumed the protection of the only two white people around. In Mompox I had seen only a couple of black faces.

The vibrancy of the riverside street was instantly catching. I was humming to myself a famous cumbia tune as we wound our way between people and vehicles, alongside a market encased in diseased yellow plaster, past shops psychedelically painted in luminous oranges, purples and blues. The interiors were dark and high-ceilinged, with slowly rotating fans and rusting shelves half-stocked with bags of beans and ancient tins. We entered one shop to buy some necessary provisions. We bought four bottles of rum, and celebrated the purchase with a bottle of chilled beer and then another. The old woman serving us was talkative and friendly, and her daughter at the till friendly and smiling. Diomidio rang me on my cellphone to see how we were. He told us again not to hurry. 'Have another beer,' he said, 'and bring me back a woman.'

We had the beer in a backstreet bar, where we had arrived dehydrated from the sauna-like heat that was building up.

Then Diomidio rang again to tell us that the boat was about to leave. We returned a different way, down a promenade parallel to the river, evocative of the one-time prosperity that Samper had foreseen. It was paved in clay tiles, planted with palms and framed by pretentious art deco villas whose newly painted plasterwork was only partly successful in disguising the promenade's general air of a place whose heyday had come and gone.

The centrepiece was a painted statue of Bolívar that the authorities had not thought of repairing in time for the bicentenary of Colombia's War of Independence. The bronze-coloured paint was peeling off like the skin of a sunburn victim and half of the Liberator's face had gone completely. A drunken hooligan had apparently taken a potshot with a gun.

Diomidio talked about Bolívar once we were back on the *Catalina* and the sailors had completed their elaborate ritual of tying and untying cables so that all our barges would be in place. The stretch of the river between Barranquilla and Magangué, where we due the next day, was apparently named after the Liberator. 'And can you guess why?' asked Diomidio. We could not. 'It's because this is the straightest and most easily navigable stretch of the river.' I still could not understand. 'Bolívar's early life', he explained, with little regard for historical accuracy, 'was one effortless triumph after the other.'

He added that this part of the Magdalena was the scene of one of the Liberator's greatest victories, 'the famous Bloodless Massacre'. 'And do you know why it was bloodless?' We did not. 'Bolívar was determined to win a battle without any blood being shed. So he ordered his generals to kill his enemies with stones and then throw the bodies into the river.' Diomidio shook with laughter as he told us this.

The *Catalina* finally cast its moorings. The weight of the additional barges slowed the boat down even further as it moved into the centre of the river, from where 'Calamar, *kilómetro* 90.7' appeared like a dainty strung-out necklace. None of the new barges was carrying anything. I was beginning to think of our journey as an allegory of futility. Julio opened the first bottle of rum and offered me a swig.

Yet another plate piled high with rice and plantains awaited us at lunch. The meat this time could have been chicken. The boat progressed in an unvarying straight line through an unvarying flat landscape compared by Isaac Holton to the 'scenery or want of scenery of the lower Mississippi'. The effects of the rum, the heat, the boat's numbing slowness, the engine's incessant roar, the overall monotony, were all converging. The memory of the brief stay in Calamar was already like the memory of a dream.

I was sleepily aware of a line of low hills on the horizon. The heat of the day was at its worst, and sweat was pouring from me even as I slumped under the awning of the gangway. There was a tap on my shoulder. Alfredo was proposing that Julio and I come with him. On a tour of inspection of the barges.

Two of the new barges, crossed by yellow pipes, had been placed side by side in front of the one carrying the tanks, beyond which were the two remaining barges, also side by side, immensely long, seeming to stretch all the way to the imperceptibly approaching hills. The tanks appeared now like enthroned deities travelling in procession. At Calamar a dozen or so miscellaneous objects had been scattered at their feet, like offerings.

Alfredo wanted Julio to record these on a sheet of paper. Julio dutifully noted down such objects as two red pumps, a pallet whose goods were hidden under wrapping, and four grey plastic flexi-tubes about eight metres long. Julio had as little idea as I had how to describe properly what we were seeing. Alfredo, in any case, did not seem to mind what Julio wrote. He never even asked to look at this amateurish inventory. The whole exercise served no apparent purpose other than as a way of Alfredo exerting his little authority, of passing the time, of trying to find meaning where there was none.

The hills, with their woods and luxuriant fields, were now flanking us on both sides. The river was narrowing. From tomorrow onwards, warned Alfredo, the navigation would become very difficult. Our first hurdle was a stretch of treacherous bends where the water level was said to have rapidly sunk over the past two weeks. He wasn't quite sure when we would get there, 'perhaps by as early as tomorrow night, perhaps in two days' time'. Tomorrow, he then added, the soldiers were arriving.

Did the dangers of an attack also increase after tomorrow? Alfredo did not really answer my question. He just said that we would be entering a part of Colombia that had known great problems in the past.

We moved onto the last two barges and proceeded towards

their tip. We were walking ever further apart. Alfredo lugubri-
ously took up the rear, while Julio was in the middle, stopping
continually to take photos. I strode far in front, feeling a
renewed sense of vulnerability. The boat seemed now an
impossibly long way behind, and had become inaudible. I felt
like a solitary intruder searching for shade and protection.

I jumped over the loudly contracting and expanding gap
separating the barge I was on from the one parallel to it. I was
drawn by a large and enigmatic enclosure entered through a
circular opening with a safe-like door. Inside was a space as
large as a football pitch, open to the sky, completely empty,
blindingly white, a world of its own within the greater
enclosed world of the *Catalina*.

The voice of Julio took me by surprise. He was speaking in
the hushed tone of an awestruck devotee in a temple. His
thoughts were the same as mine. He said we had found the
perfect hiding-place, 'should anything happen'.

Heat exhaustion, mosquito bites and endless delays on sandbanks were the most likely dangers in the post-colonial days
of passenger travel up the Magdalena. And boredom. Almost
every account I had read of the journey mentioned at some
stage the boredom. Boredom caused by the interminably slow
pace, the unchanging landscapes, the monotonous bad food,
the lack of a good book to read, the forced interaction with
people with whom you had nothing in common other than a
shared sense of boredom.

I was mulling this over in my over-air-conditioned cabin,
after a short afternoon siesta. I raised my head to peer out of

the porthole. The hills had gone, and the river seemed once again as wide as it had been before Calamar. I looked at my watch: it was nearly 4.30, supper would be almost ready. I anticipated an evening almost identical to yesterday's, future days on the boat no different to the one that was almost over. Yet I still could not imagine myself ever becoming bored.

Humboldt had never complained of boredom. He was one of my mentors, a man of superhuman energy and curiosity who had travelled up the Magdalena in a state of constant wonderment, never complaining, never ill, never tired. But the person I was thinking of in particular as I gradually rose from my bunk was my Uncle Brendan, my father's only sibling. He too had had an extraordinary capacity for making the most of every situation, for finding interest in everyone and everything.

Brendan had been the older and luckier of the two brothers. His life, lived mainly as a GP in the Nottingham suburb of Arnold, might have lacked the glamorous episodes of my father's. But his mind had remained intact and open to new experiences almost up to the time he died, a few weeks short of his ninety-first birthday, three weeks before I had come to Colombia.

I had been present at his deathbed, but I still could not accept that he was dead. I thought about him every day. I was storing up tales about Diomidio and others to tell him on my return to Europe. I also needed to talk to him about my mother, just as I had always turned to him for help during my father's disturbing decline. He had once offered me what was perhaps the only possible advice for someone witnessing the slow disappearance of a mind: to enjoy one's own life with added intensity.

'Migueleeeto,' cried Diomidio, looking up from his plate of rice and plantain as I entered the dining-room. He had been waiting for this moment. He was almost desperate to hand over to me a document he had printed off from his rudimentary computer. It was a list of every community along the navigable stretch of the Magdalena, together, of course, with its exact distance from Barranquilla.

After lunch, I took it with me to my seat on the gangway. I had also brought along García Márquez's *Love in the Time of Cholera*, his meditation on the persistence of love over the years, part of which was set on a steamship travelling up the Magdalena. I had thought of this as the ideal read for the trip, a necessary reminder of the river as a source of passion and magic. But, as with all the books that weighed down my luggage whenever I travelled, I had yet to get further than the first page. There was so much to distract me on the journey.

I now tried reading more of the book, but I kept on looking up at the river's banks. They might not have changed much, but there was always some new detail to observe, the canoe gliding out from the rushes, the floating oil barrel, the swarm of birds gathering around the pink blossom of a tree. Through a mysterious trail of association, I found myself remembering a university lecturer's description of Velázquez's *Las Meninas*, my favourite painting. The lecturer was a dithery, absentminded old man whom everyone made fun of, but few people understood. His words about the painting, coming back to me in the context of the Magdalena, seemed now more profound and apt than ever: 'Nothing is happening, but in a sense everything is happening.'

The list of places Diomidio had given me provided further diversion. Julio, sitting beside me, was engrossed by this as well. We took it in turns to read out the many implausible-sounding but officially recognized names of the places we would be passing. Together they read like the stream-of-consciousness utterances of a surrealist performance. An encapsulation of all human experience.

Purgatory, The Snorer, Whirlpool of Death, The Happy Man, Mosquito Point, Hanged Man's Hill, Happiness, The Quiet Life, Such is Life, Sausages, Belly Gut, Silence, Death's Coffer, Lighting and Shadows, The Woman with the Red Trousers, Witches, Last Resort, Big Fanny. 'La Chucha Gorda, *kilómetro* 165.8,' corrected Diomidio, who had crept up behind us and couldn't resist intervening on hearing the last name. He wanted us to be true sailors and learn all the distances. He also insisted on the seriousness of the names. They were, he said, like a Morse code that kept alive the memory of the Magdalena's legends and history.

Big Fanny was a place where a young woman with 'an enormous fanny' was once caught having a shower. The Woman with the Red Trousers referred to a woman who was always seen washing a pair of red trousers whenever a boat passed. Hanged Man's Hill was a renowned suicide spot. Whirlpool of Death was the site of a whirlpool that had swallowed up a whole ship. Diomidio added that a phantom ship still haunted the area. He claimed to have seen it twenty years ago.

And where did he think we would reach by nightfall? He wasn't quite sure. He doubted we would get much beyond Purgatory.

7

A series of broken calls from London came through on my phone in the hour before sunset. My mother was back from hospital, but refusing to eat or drink. Ten minutes later I heard she had had a glass of milk. A few minutes afterwards she had managed half a yoghurt. She had then tried eating a grape but had given up. My brother had cut short a meeting in Strasbourg and was on his way to see her. After that I couldn't get a signal. Diomidio didn't think there would be another one until way after Purgatory, 'if at all'. He said we were entering a black hole where even the most up-to-date technology began inexplicably to fail.

Rum and the sunset helped briefly to take my mind off my mother. I was once again with Julio at the lonely head of our procession of barges. Sailors had already come to place the tripod and its lantern, and had gone. We took turns with the bottle of rum as we squatted almost at the water's edge.

The sun was setting before us. The evening before it had quietly faded into the gloom like a candle slowly burning out. Today it was saying its farewell with the furious look of a bonfire on which fuel had been poured. A tiny fishing boat was racing home, its net raised as if in horror against a sky of blackened and burning clouds. The flames spread everywhere, intensified and then were spent.

We advanced in the afterglow towards Plató, already one of the distant-seeming memories from my journey to Mompox. I thought of the *hombre caimán,* now surely asleep, as we sailed beneath the town's suspension bridge, towards the lights of Purgatory. The lights came and went, and still the boat continued, under a now pitch-black and moonless sky. Diomidio had apparently decided to sail on regardless of conditions, to have another night without stopping. Or perhaps the decision had not been his at all. The *Catalina*'s movements seemed governed less and less by human reason.

Julio and I remained where we were, transfixed by the void, hoping to stay up late enough to reach the Whirlpool of Death. We were rational and sceptical beings, yet we secretly believed in the existence of the phantom ship and that we would be bound to see it.

We waited until well past midnight. The silence and darkness were finally broken. We heard a strange rumble and glimpsed a flashing light. It took a few anxious moments to realize what was happening. My phone had made a brief and unexpected sign of life. I had received a text message. My mother had got through a bowl of cornflakes.

'Did you get to see the phantom ship?' asked Juan Cano, giving me a smile laced with irony. We were mooring just after breakfast at 'Yatí, *kilómetro* 233.9,' a village with an army base four kilometres from Magangué. Juan Cano stood with me on the gangway watching us pull up next to a dark-red tugboat that stained the limpid early morning landscape like a pool of blood. A distinct complicity was building up between us, though a mutual shyness had so far held us back from anything more than a few brief exchanges. He shared a similar dry sense of humour, and made me feel I could trust him far more than I could his superiors. I saw in him an underlying seriousness, together with the stoical resignation of someone who knew that he deserved a more rewarding life than that of a poorly paid pilot on an apparent path to nowhere.

I was beginning to know the crew slightly better, to find out more about their individual stories and personalities. The sailors lingered that tiny bit longer as they coincided with Julio and me on the gangway. They seemed to want to unburden themselves to us. We appeared to project for them the wisdom and privilege of people who existed in a world beyond that of the boat. We were undoubted objects of curiosity. One of them even wondered if I was the author of *Love in the Time of Cholera*. He couldn't imagine any other reason for my having a copy of the book with me.

Nearly all of the sailors were from places we had seen or were going to see along the river. One of the *Catalina*'s cooks,

Leiva, was from Yatí. He intended making use of our brief stop
here to visit members of his family, with whom he spent barely
two weeks a year. He was ordered by Diomidio to take us with
him. We felt guilty at intruding upon his precious family time,
yet he said he welcomed the opportunity to talk to us and to
show off his 'beautiful village'. We walked towards its centre
along a muddy riverside path.

Leiva was an unmarried man in his early forties, with a high
forehead and a solemn air. He had once thought of joining the
Colombian Army, he told us as we passed the local barracks,
eight of whose soldiers were on the point of boarding the
Catalina. But his real vocation had always been in the kitchen.
He hoped one day to have his own establishment. He considered his twenty years of working for the Naviera Fluvial as a
necessary if rather over-protracted apprenticeship.

Beyond the neatly landscaped barracks was the village
proper, a confusion of rutted tracks scattered with brightly
coloured homes in concrete and corrugated iron. Leiva's
mother lived opposite a large and uncared-for cemetery 'full of
victims from the troubles'. Two of his sisters had houses along
a street where pigs ran loose. We finished our tour in a
bamboo-covered eatery down by the river, alongside a trench
where a couple of donkeys grazed among discarded plastic
bottles. Leiva said that his real dream was to own a place such
as this, in his home village. He would then think about marrying and settling down. He confessed he was finding it ever
more difficult to tear himself away from here.

The soldiers were well ensconced in the *Catalina* when we
got back. Their commander, a surly man in his thirties, was

seated with a laptop at our dining table, scrolling the screen
distractedly for no apparent purpose. Four of his underlings
were sprawled on chairs watching the barely functioning
television. They seemed bored before their journey had even
begun. The sole response to the actual moment of departure
was to turn up the television's volume to a degree that its dis-
tortions were unbearable. Not one of the soldiers' heads
turned as we sailed past Magangué, a fleeting vision of the
modern urban world, with concrete apartments, a satellite dish
like a flying saucer and a compellingly tall twin-towered cathedral in white and cream. Their eyes remained blankly glued to
a television whose blizzard-like images were as unpredictable
as the signal on my mobile. They were looking at children's
cartoons.

Julio escaped eventually to the bridge, where I too soon
took refuge from the invaders. I found him there on his own
with Juan Cano, listening with a smile to tales about our captain. Juan Cano spoke of Diomidio as an amiable figure of fun
whose most recent absurdity was his claim to have improved
the boat's computer by installing on it 'Windows 20', a non-
existent program.

'And he always insists he's right, he seems genuinely to
believe in his fantasies,' murmured Juan Cano, his hands grip-
ping the rudder, his serious expression shading into a slight
grin as he went on to recall the captain's sightings of the platypus and the phantom ship. 'The phantom ship, the phantom
ship,' he repeated in a tone of gentle mockery that almost
became one of wistfulness. 'I would so love to see it.'

*

I was resting again in my bunk during the worst heat of the afternoon. I was half asleep, dreamily picturing the phantom ship as the stranded Spanish galleon in *One Hundred Years of Solitude*, the gold-encrusted apparition which appears in the jungle between Macondo and the sea. The ship that would become for literary critics the defining image of magical realism. Was this perhaps what Diomidio had seen on the Magdalena? As I wondered about this I thought again of the fifteen-year-old García Márquez as he journeyed upriver for the first time. He had only just boarded the *David Arango*, having travelled from Barranquilla to Magangué in a small launch accompanied at the last minute by his adventure-loving father. The father had finally left. His fifteen-year-old son was experiencing what solitude was truly like. Unable to face the first night's supper and orchestral ball, he went out onto the deck, where he stood for ages on his own. He watched the disappearing lights of the world before retiring to a cabin he shared with a ferocious-looking giant who carried with him a case of knives and was known to everyone as Jack the Ripper. The young García Márquez cried until dawn.

But, by the second day, the journey was already changing for him into a continuous floating fiesta, animated by music-loving students, heightened by exotic sights and fragrances. The ship was a treasure trove of future memories, full of novelistic personalities as unforgettable as its captain, an authoritative figure with a gigantic appetite and a name as sonorous as Diomidio's: Clímaco Conde Abello.

The captain was engaged in a quixotic struggle to save the wildlife of the Magdalena. He said if you killed off the river's animals the whole world would die. He would be perennially associated in García Márquez's mind with the journey's most memorable incident, the rescue one night of a female manatee who had got caught up in branches along the river's bank. The creature, as strange and mythical-seeming as Diomidio's platypus, was nearly four metres long and looked like a cross between a cow and a woman.

Her wails would merge in García Márquez's memory with the constant singing of boleros and the strains of an instrument he would have loved to have possessed, an accordion, played masterfully on the boat by a young man whom he began greatly to envy. Though they never spoke, his recollection of this person was so intense that, thirty years later, he was able to pick him out among the participants of a neurology conference in Paris. The former accordionist, Salomón Hakim, had turned into a world-famous neurosurgeon who had launched his medical career by performing necropsies on Alzheimer's patients.

There was one other passenger whom García Márquez would always remember, 'the insatiable reader', a bespectacled, prematurely balding man who stood out by making no attempt to speak to anyone and sitting always at the furthest table in the dining-room, reading a new book each day. García Márquez glanced furtively at the titles, registering Alain-Fournier's *Le Grand Meaulnes*, a favourite novel of his and of every bookish adolescent, a work to encourage not only romantic passion, but also a belief in the existence of magical realms.

The fantastical costume party that forms the centrepiece of

Le Grand Meaulnes was how I imagined García Márquez's days on the *David Arango*. It was also how I came to remember an experience that took place only a few days after my nervous farewell to my parents at Victoria Station.

I had stumbled upon a group of after-lunch revellers in the middle of the Andalucian countryside. I was called over to have a glass of Montilla wine and then another one. I went up to an old gypsy who was said to have known the poet Federico García Lorca. A group of singing students drove me off in the evening to an enchanted castle on a hill. I met a beautiful young woman with whom I promised to remain in touch but never did.

I had woken up the next morning without a hangover, but with a sense of having had a special experience that alcohol alone could not explain. This pleasant feeling faded quickly as the day advanced, but I was left with an emotion that would never go: a longing to try and recreate the memory.

What the *Catalina* really lacked, admitted one of the sailors, was the presence of women. A woman cook had once been employed, but that 'hadn't worked out too well'. She had never returned, said the sailor, taking another swig at the bottle of rum that was being passed around by Julio.

We were having a secret little party at the end of the barges. Julio had an anarchic streak, and a way of making life slightly easier for everyone. He had already exploited our new intimacy with Leiva to have our supper kept warm for us in the kitchen, so that we could eat it at a more reasonable hour. As for the rum, he had noticed how the sailors were reluctant to drink any on the boat itself, as they were technically not supposed to do so. So he suggested that they came to what was now our favourite evening spot – a small hidden stretch of deck at the far tip of our floating world.

Four of the young sailors had timidly turned up. I had secretly hoped for some music, the playing of an accordion, the singing of boleros or *vallenatos*. But instead all that was on offer was conversation and drink. The conversation was elemental in its topics. We began with sex, and then moved on to death. I learnt every Colombian term for female genitalia, and heard about two gruesome accidents witnessed by the sailors, 'more or less from where we are now'.

Both accidents had involved small vessels that had collided with the tugboat and its cargo and been sucked below the surface. In one case a soldier had simply lost control of his launch when the engine had failed. 'His body was never recovered.' The other disaster had had even more serious consequences, and had occurred on the *Catalina*'s last voyage upriver, 'about five weeks ago'. A motorized canoe, travelling at night, had struck the furthest barge. 'All eight of its passengers were killed.'

The sailors said that accidents of this kind were unfortunately only too common and *chalupas* were particularly prone to them. Furthermore, your chances of survival after falling into the river were slim. Though you would be extremely unlucky today to be eaten by a caiman, you were very likely to be drowned by the powerful currents and whirlpools. 'And if you manage to get out of the river alive, you need to have your stomach pumped immediately.' I remembered a story told by García Márquez of how a couple of guerrillas, escaping from the Army, had jumped into the river and had later died from the effects of the polluted waters.

A *chalupa* slid past us in the dusk, silently, almost invisibly. Vessels other than tugboats were not officially allowed to travel after dark, but no one appeared to pay much attention to this rule. 'There are lots of laws in Colombia, but no one obeys them,' smiled Julio, handing me the rum. The sailors agreed, while recognizing the common sense behind many of these rules. For instance, sailing at night up the Magdalena on a small vessel was extremely dangerous, 'especially when completely pissed'.

Everyone in the canoe that had hit the *Catalina* had apparently been drunk. We were near the site where the accident had happened. The moon had yet to rise and the only light now was that of our boat. 'We're there,' said one of the sailors, pointing towards the total darkness. How he could tell where we were was a mystery to me, but none of his companions disputed him. They all stared in the same direction, respectfully silent for a few moments. Then someone mentioned that one of the victims had been a paramilitary. 'That complicated matters.'

I asked him why. 'The paramilitaries never forgive if one of their companions dies. They'll be blaming the Naviera Fluvial for the accident. They'll be wanting their revenge.' He didn't believe that the Magdalena today was as safe as people said it was. Attacks on boats were unlikely, but still possible. 'Nowhere in Colombia is completely safe.' No one wanted any more rum. The sailors said that they had to get back on duty. We would be arriving soon at the place where we would be mooring for the night. We couldn't go on any further because we were about to reach the challenging stretch of the river that Alfredo had told us about. It had to be negotiated by daylight. The slightest mistake could be critical.

The sailors went, the party was over. The river's dark and silent banks, monitoring our progress with their unseen presences, were becoming clearer under the light of the finally appearing moon, a near-perfect full moon. They seemed closer than before and impenetrably wooded. And they were performing the unexpected. They were beginning to curve.

We were moored in the middle of nowhere, at a hamlet whose name I did not bother to ask. 'As you ascend the river,' wrote Isaac Holton in 1857, 'the villages grow smaller and you forget to inquire their names.' The place where we had stopped for the night could not have had more than three or four houses, only one of which was visible, a distant glow among the trees.

A few of the local inhabitants, perhaps all of them, had stepped onto the front two barges, and were trying to sell fish to the crew. Alfredo was simultaneously bargaining and flirting with a pretty girl who could hardly have been more than fifteen. When I came up to them, they reached a quick deal and the girl ran off, to catch up with her departing companions. 'She was a sharp one,' Alfredo muttered, complaining of the 'outrageous price' he had finally agreed to. He went off disgruntled to his bed. 'It's a big day tomorrow.'

The rest of the crew soon followed suit, except for one of the boat's two elderly pilots, Pacho, a burly, shaven-headed man whom I had imagined as a knife thrower in a circus, like García Márquez's cabin mate on the *David Arango*. He was sitting with Julio on one of the barge's yellow pipes. He gestured to me to come over. He said he was telling Julio about his life, another sad and frustrated one, to judge by the way Julio had been shaking his head in sympathy. He repeated part of the story for my benefit.

'I was never cut out to be a sailor,' he began. 'I would never have imagined doing what I do now when I was younger. I'm a city man, a typical Barranquillero. I used to love dancing, having a good time, being with women. Then I married and got myself a job as a clerk in a distillery. I was still happy, in fact happier than ever. I had a reasonable income and plenty of time to be with my family. I didn't want anything else. And then I was sacked.'

He was sacked for being 'too honest'. He had reported crates of alcohol regularly going missing. His boss told him not to worry, the quantity wasn't that great. But he persisted. It was obvious that someone high up in the firm was siphoning off the alcohol. When they silenced him by getting rid of him ('a model employee for over twenty years'), there was no other job he could do. And then he was taken on by the Naviera Fluvial ('no women, no dancing, no time with the family, no money to speak of'). He had been with them for over half his life. Like Diomidio, he couldn't wait to retire. He had only two more years to go.

'That's Colombia, isn't it?' he concluded, turning to Julio for approbation. 'It's the most beautiful country in the world, and it's also the most tragic.'

It was almost midnight and everyone on the boat was asleep, even the two soldiers on night duty, both of whom were gently snoring on the gangway, their machine guns on the point of falling off their laps. I was not yet ready for my cabin. I had anticipated dropping into my bunk in a rum-induced stupor, but the boat's atmosphere of melancholy and foreboding had kept me sober and awake. I was also worrying about my mother. I had spent much of the day doing so.

I had managed to contact London three more times since the momentous news of her cornflakes consumption. She was still hardly eating or drinking. A doctor had visited and pronounced her fine, but I feared that some remaining strand of rationality in her had decided that she had had enough and that she had made a conscious decision to give up living. I had yet to speak to my brother, though I had had an upsetting conversation with my mother's oldest neighbour, normally the most phlegmatic person, but now quite emotional. She had been obviously shocked at seeing the dignified, appearance-conscious person she had known lying on top of her bed in a torn nightie screaming at everyone to go away. The neighbour hoped I would be back from Colombia soon.

I leant against the railings of the gangway, looking down at fast-flowing waters that seemed to contain all memories. As they glistened now under the bright moonlight, they carried me to a place far away from Colombia, to another time of day and a different era. I saw my mother as a young woman on a Mediterranean shoreline, laughing with friends, running across sunlit sands towards a limpid blue sea.

The Mediterranean would always be my mother's lifeline. She needed to see it at least once a year, to bathe in its waters, to relax reading on one of its beaches. When my father became incapable of travelling, she put him into care for the first time, for a ten-day spell that allowed her to visit a Turkish resort. She defended her action on the grounds that without her annual contact with the Mediterranean she wouldn't be able to look after my father at all and would be dead long before him. The sea held for her miraculous powers of rejuvenation.

This obsession went back to the time her parents moved to the Sicilian coastal town of Messina. Her years in Messina became in memory as magical as García Márquez's early experiences on the Magdalena. She spoke of them as if they had been one continuous sunny afternoon on the beach. She was on the beach when she should have been studying for law exams at the university. She was on the beach when she was spotted by the celebrated theatre director and playwright Eduardo De Filippo. She was persuaded by him to give up the law and become an actor in his company.

In later life, when my mother talked about her youth in Messina, she loved projecting an image of herself as a striking, carefree beauty constantly surrounded on the beach by male admirers. Yet until the age of twenty-four, when she met my father, she appears never to have fallen for anyone. The only admirer of hers she ever mentioned was someone called Pippo, an enormously tall man whom everyone in her family thought she would marry. He was totally in love with her, he followed her everywhere, he accompanied her to the beach. He was a kind and generous friend whom she said she found an embarrassment.

Pippo never forgot her. He would never love anyone else. He would remain an unmarried man who stayed in touch with my mother for the rest of his life. I remember him as a smiling man with greased-back hair who turned up at my grand-parents' home in Genoa carrying a bag of sweets for 'the boys'. He died, curiously, the same day as my father, 10 July 1997. News of Pippo's death affected my mother almost more than her immediate grief, for which she had been long prepared. She felt as García Márquez had on hearing of the burning of the *David Arango*. A last link with her youth had gone.

8

The boat was moving again when I got up in the morning. It was 6 a.m. and Julio was already on the bridge, watching a solitary sailor walking towards the end of the barges with a huge pole.

The two tanks no longer obstructed the view. Julio said that we had left them behind at our nameless night-stop because the tugboat was incapable of pushing its full load up this difficult stretch of the river. We would return for them once we had deposited the four empty barges twenty-five kilometres upstream, at a place called Armenia. Going to Armenia, returning for the tanks, and then going back again to Armenia to reunite our full cargo, would apparently take up the greater part of the day, 'if we were lucky'.

A hydraulics engineer from Bogotá, an earnest-looking man with glasses, had joined us for this notoriously complicated stretch of the Magdalena. He had been contracted by the

Naviera Fluvial to make an assessment of the river's current water levels. He appeared to have brought little with him other than a notebook, a pencil and a chart.

He showed me on the chart the dramatic two horseshoe bends we were about to undertake. He explained that the continually shifting sediment on the river's banks made sonar soundings extremely difficult, even if each barge were to be equipped with the instrument needed for such soundings. And what about the state-of-art technology that Hector had been so proud of? 'More or less useless,' he said. 'When it comes to awkward stretches such as these, you have to depend mainly on trial and error, and, of course, on the pole. Just as in the old days.'

The sailor with the pole was in position and waving back to Juan Cano to tell him so. The sailor leant precariously with the pole over the side of one barge and plunged it into the water to a depth of about four metres. Then he crossed over into the adjacent barge and did the same on the opposite side. He gave Juan Cano the thumbs-up sign. We travelled on for another fifty metres, then the sailor repeated the whole operation. We were moving at about seven kilometres an hour. The early Spanish explorers had probably made better and more secure progress on a *champán*.

One of the few modern tools that appeared to be working was my cellphone. It was the only cellphone on board to have a signal. It defied the prevailing wisdom that we had entered a signal-free zone by ringing loudly and insistently. I feared the worst.

My mother had gone mad. Her cleaner thought she might

calm down by speaking to me, but she became worse still, pouring out a random stream of abuse. She seemed to think I was her husband and I had abandoned her. When I told her that the man she was thinking of had been dead for over thirteen years, she wished I had been the one who had died and not her husband. 'He was always such a good man,' she shouted, 'while you were always the bad one. You haven't changed at all over the years. You've now sent a group of women to poison me.' I tried hard to convince her that I was her beloved younger son, and that she would be seeing me again 'shortly', perhaps in less than a month. *'I'll be dead by then!'* she screamed in a voice so loud that even Julio could hear her. 'You've been such a disappointment to me, such a disappointment ...'

I couldn't make out anything else. The signal weakened and then died completely. In that moment I did not want it to return. I wished for the days when the only way of being contacted abroad was through a letter sent to a *poste restante*. I almost wished for the days of Humboldt, when something terrible could happen to a member of your family and you wouldn't hear about it until a year or two later. Julio suggested giving up the journey when we got to Barrancabermeja, from where I could easily fly back to Bogotá and from there to Europe. I said I'd wait and see. There was a side to me that believed that this recent crisis with my mother was just an attention-seeking ploy, a reawakening of the actor within her. There was another side racked with guilt.

At the rate we were travelling we would never even reach Barrancabermeja. We appeared to be going in circles. The dramatic bends in the river were disorienting, especially now that the trees had thinned out along the banks, allowing regular sightings across fields and swamps of a church tower that was visible one moment on one side of the boat and then on the other, seemingly ever closer, then ever further, and vice versa. Thus, when I thought we had finally said goodbye to the building, it was suddenly right next to us again, two hours later.

The church belonged to a village called Pinillos, 'Pinillos, *kilómetro* 299.3.' The voice was that of Diomidio, next to us on the bridge and letting it be known that this village of seemingly no more than a church and a few shacks was a sort of Cambridge of the Magdalena estuary, a major place of learning.

Diomidio had today become more expansive than ever. He was also dressed differently. He had jettisoned his green overalls in favour of a showy, striped brown shirt, open almost to the navel to expose hanging from his neck what looked like the contents of a silver vault. Today was his big day as a captain, and he was enjoying playing it up in front of Julio and me, posing for photos as if he were a celebrity arriving at a gala event.

At times he reminded me of an orchestra conductor I had known, so fat he could barely move but managing to keep going by taking repeated rests on a high stool, and getting up only in moments of significantly increased tempo or to receive the applause of the audience.

The Magdalena itself was coming to resemble a complex piece of music, slow and sinuous, with endlessly recurring leitmotifs, as well as many variations in the form of all the new waterways that had begun to join ours, including those of the Loba, the Palomino and the Cauca. Diomidio and other members of the crew gave us ample warning as we approached the mouth of each of these main rivers. The moment of passing them counted as a crescendo.

I managed nonetheless to miss the Boca del Cauca, at least the first time round. I was on the wrong side of the boat and distracted by thoughts of my mother. But I got to see it the second time we passed, as we sailed downriver to pick up the tanks. The Cauca is Colombia's second largest river and has suffered as much as the Magdalena during the years of fighting between guerrillas, paramilitaries and the Army. Julio poetically envisaged the meeting of the two rivers as a powerful collision of reds rather than as what it actually was – an innocuous convergence of clearer and more greenish waters with those that were murkier and browner.

However, we did see near the mouth a sight that caused a slight shiver. Julio mistook it at first for the corpse of a man, but in fact it was that of a pig. A floating pig pecked at by vultures.

We were soon preparing ourselves for the day's last challenge: to see the tanks successfully through what Julio and I had dubbed the Bends of Pinillos. The journey to Armenia and back had so far been accomplished laboriously but with relative ease. However, the engineer from Bogotá was concerned about the water level. He thought it low enough to create serious problems for the tanks: he estimated their chances of continuing upriver as 'fifty-fifty'. Diomidio was more optimistic, and whispered in my ear that 'the people of Bogotá never have a clue'. Alfredo, meanwhile, was still worrying about the fish he had bought last night and which we had eaten for lunch. 'Tasty but too expensive, just like the girl who sold it to me.'

An atmosphere of tension began to engulf the whole boat. The sailor with the pole was standing by the side of one of the tanks and shaking his head. The boat was progressing a few hundred metres before getting stuck for ever longer periods of time, and then moving back again. Alfredo had a look of morose resignation, while Diomidio was gesturing frantically before storming out of the bridge. The Bogotá man was smugly writing down some notes.

We managed to keep going for a while by moving in zig-zag fashion, but then we came to what I was convinced was a terminal halt. I went for a stroll on the gangway, where I encountered Leiva. I asked him what would happen next. He said we would have to wait for the water level to rise. He said that Medellín was already experiencing the first storms of the season, so perhaps the delay wouldn't be too great. 'Maybe a day, maybe two. Maybe even a week.'

Diomidio hadn't given up. He had taken control of the pole himself and was rushing all over the place, testing the depth of the water, signalling back to Juan Cano, shouting to the other sailors. He had become once again the conductor, determined to recapture the attention of his audience with one stirring, unforgettable finale, the consecration of his whole career. He was perspiring so much that his body appeared to be melting. Dark patches of sweat were spreading under his arms. He

paused continually to recover his breath. I feared he would
have a heart attack.

The boat shifted and continued advancing in a straight line.
Diomidio jumped in the air with joy. He waved frantically
when he saw me. '*Migueleeeto!*' he shouted as loud as he
could. 'We've made it! We've made it!' He was genuinely
incredulous. He skipped all the way back to the boat. The slap
of his hand against mine almost knocked me to the ground.

Alfredo, who had done nothing, responded more soberly –
with his whole philosophy of life. The philosophy consisted of
just three words, 'Persist, insist, resist.' Diomidio, in a double
act with Alfredo, started chanted the words repeatedly, and
then persuaded Julio and I to join in. 'Persist, insist, resist. And
all together now. Persist, insist, resist. Persist, insist, resist.
Persist, insist, resist ...'

A motorized canoe sailed past towards evening. It was the
flimsiest of vessels, carrying around thirty passengers, crowded
together under the shade of a black tarpaulin almost blown off
by the warm wind. I was struck by its name, apparently that
of the village it was from: *La Vida Cambia*, 'Life Changes'.

Life on the *Catalina*, after the crisis of the early afternoon,
had superficially changed little. We were once more pushing
the full contingent of barges. The engineer from Bogotá had
gone. Diomidio was wearing his overalls again, and five of the
soldiers were sitting stupefied in front of the television.

I was back with Julio in our usual evening spot, only partly
reassured by the latest news of my mother. She had been visited
by another doctor, who had found her calm and in 'surprisingly

good health'. But recently I had also been told that her brain scans had merely shown 'normal brain cell degeneration'. I no longer believed anything that was said about her. I saw her as having reached a stage of existence where rational analysis of her condition was as ineffective as the sonar soundings on the Magdalena.

The further I travelled upriver, the more I seemed afflicted by the journey's underlying sense of uncertainty. The more, too, I was appreciating the soothing powers of nature, which were once again beginning to work their spell as the colours of the landscape deepened, and the Magdalena woke up from its mid-afternoon siesta.

Herons, perched on floating logs, prepared to take off into a sky already streaked by flocks of geese and white egrets. Black ducks swarmed around the gaunt branches of an immensely tall tree flanked by clusters of palms. Oxen grazed on the bright green grass, and luxuriant woods were reappearing in the distance. Still further away I spotted the pale-blue profile of a smooth-ridged mountain, which Julio thought must be the Banco del Magdalena. He said that the mountain had seen some of the worst fighting in the troubles. Now it appeared as the completing element in an idyllic composition painted by an Italianate master of old.

The four sailors from yesterday arrived for their furtive swigs of rum. The latest news from the bridge was that we would again be sailing throughout the night, to make up for lost time. When I asked them for help in identifying the flora and fauna they started talking all at once. Instead of the Colombian slang for vulva, they started teaching me the names of the exotic birds and trees all around us.

I learnt that the white egrets were referred to by their Indian name of *yuyu*, and that the black ones were black-bellied whistling ducks or *pisingos*. The broadly spreading trees with their occasional buttress roots were mainly varieties of the *ceiba* – the emerald-green witch ceiba, the yellow ceiba, the white ceiba, the corkspur coral ceiba. The tall, gaunt trees were strangler figs; the shorter trees sprouting a fountain of long green leaves were cucumber trees; the ones with the pale-edged leaves were cabbage bark trees; and those with the white flowers were *guásimos* and were used for the dying of leather. 'And what about that one over there?' intervened Julio, pointing to a tree we were seeing for the first time, whose deep pink blossom outshone all its stunning competitors. 'Oh, that's a *cañandonga*,' said the sailors in unison, as if acknowledging the arrival in our midst of a celebrated beauty.

The excitement of the first Western scientists at coming across this world of unfamiliar sights and untranslatable names became almost palpable for me. I could clearly picture José Celestino Mutis, the Spanish priest and botanist, struggling up the Magdalena in 1761 to declare that all the river's ceaseless dangers and hardships were outweighed by its immeasurable benefits for science – a moment of realization that became the germ for one of the most ambitious botanical surveys ever mounted. I felt closer than ever now to my hero Humboldt. I could see him accumulating mountains of notes to discuss with Mutis at the end of a river journey that would almost kill from exhaustion his inseparable botanist companion Aimé Bonpland.

The spell I was under lasted until shortly after sunset, a sunset different from the others we had seen so far, with clouds mushrooming like explosions behind the black profiles of palms and pleading outstretched branches. It was an ominous sight. I would come to associate it with what Julio and I referred to as 'the incident with the turtle'.

'The incident with the turtle' reminded me of the guilt I had felt after eating the iguana eggs. Yet it later became so blown out of proportion in my imagination that I would end up comparing it to the futile killing of the albatross in Coleridge's *Ancient Mariner*.

We were stepping back in darkness onto the boat when one of the sailors asked me if I had ever eaten a turtle. I remembered the island near Mompox, where the sight of the stewing turtle had filled me with a gastronomic curiosity hitherto unconfessed until this moment. Julio, oblivious of the conversation, went off to the bridge, while the sailor took me into the kitchen.

He had found the turtle earlier in the day, and had kept it alive in a water-filled Tupperware bowl. He offered to prepare it for me for tomorrow night's supper. He said the meat was much more tender and flavoursome if left to marinade for a day in a mixture of rum, corn oil and spices. What happened next was something Julio admitted he was glad not to have witnessed.

The sailor took out a cleaver from a drawer and, with his free hand, held the turtle down against a chopping board. The turtle retreated into his shell, but was probably not expecting the blow to come from where it did. The cleaver smashed right down onto the shell, breaking it in two. I quickly averted my eyes, but the noise of the splitting shell was unforgettable. I thought of a friend who had had a pet turtle for forty-eight years, ever since she was a young child. The pet, known as Lettuce, would probably outlive her. The turtle whose death I had just been party to would probably have outlived all of us on the *Catalina*. I would never even get to eat it.

9

I was in a deep sleep when Julio tapped me on the shoulder. I shrieked as if someone had come to murder me. He was trying to persuade me to get dressed as soon as I could and go out onto the deck. He said that today's dawn was the most beautiful yet and he didn't want me to miss it. 'You'll never guess where we are,' he added, as I rubbed my eyes and gradually became fully conscious. I couldn't guess, nor could I believe him when he told me. We were approaching Último Caso, a village whose name had set us dreaming ever since we'd seen it on Diomidio's list, a name with numerous connotations of finality – the last resort, the final example, the last man on earth, the last lunatic, the end of the line.

Julio was right about the dawn. A fading full moon hung high over a cloudless pale-blue sky tinged the faintest pink. There was a reviving freshness in the air and the promise of a joyous day ahead. A middle-aged Popeye lookalike, with bulging arms attached to a gangly body, was whistling as he washed down the deck in a pair of technicolour Bermudas. He shook my hand vigorously and proudly announced he was celebrating his fifty-seventh birthday today.

Everyone seemed in unusually high spirits. The soldiers smiled at me for the first time, and Leiva had departed from his monotonous culinary routine by preparing my favourite Colombian breakfast of fried eggs wrapped in corn cakes. Up on the bridge, the normally taciturn elderly pilot brimmed with good cheer as he talked about his twenty-six years of service with the Naviera Fluvial.

Último Caso, a dozen or so corrugated-iron roofs below an isolated hill, was followed soon afterwards by Campo Alegre, 'Happy Field', a place which the pilot had known well during its prosperous days as a port serving the coal mines. As he indicated the spot where a coal barge still lay submerged under the river, a mountain range appeared as if by miracle behind it. It was far too high to be the Banco del Magdalena, and its summit was streaked by snow. I realized the full extent of my geographical disorientation on being told that it was the Sierra Nevada de Santa Marta. 'A magnificent range,' commented the pilot.

I was still taking it in, and wondering how we could have spent four days reaching a range within sight of our starting-point at Barranquilla, when other faraway mountains were exposed by the sun's tentative first rays. The pilot explained that we were leaving behind the great estuary of the Magdalena and entering the broad valley that split the Colombian Andes into its eastern and central ranges. The sense of having been drifting up till now in a geographical vacuum was succeeded by a feeling of purposeful, invigorating progression towards some definite goal.

With the fast-rising sun, and the first glimpses of the Andes, a party mood began building up on the *Catalina*. Diomidio was singing out my name as he emerged from his cabin, while Juan Cano greeted me with a slap on my shoulder. Down on the deck, his bronzed bald head shining in the sun, Pacho was cleaning and gutting fish with Rabelaisian relish. Julio and I, observed by the laughing Popeye, used the same hose to wash our clothes, which we then hung out to dry along the railings. We could have been adorning the boat with festive rows of streamers.

The greens along the banks were becoming a brilliant emerald, and the sky was as blue as the clearest of seas. The central range of the Andes was approaching across woods and fields to our right. The eastern one formed an inviting silhouette on the horizon in front of us. It was one of those days my mother used to describe as making you feel happy to be alive. It was a glorious start to what Julio would call the beginning of the end. The unexpected end of our stay on the *Catalina*.

The first slight feelings of unease came during our mid-morning lunch. Alfredo, after crossing himself as usual before eating, launched into a subject he thought appropriate to the mood of good cheer that had infected the boat: women and sex. We were due to stop that night outside a town whose name sounded suitably vice-ridden: Gamarra. 'The women of

Gamarra,' sighed Alfredo, 'you've never met any women like them.' 'Better than the ones of Calamar?' I asked. My irony went undetected. 'They're in a category of their own,' confirmed Diomidio, who now appeared set on taking Julio and me to a special place in Gamarra where we were bound 'to have lots of fun'.

The prospect of a night of prostitutes with Diomidio and Alfredo did not have the effect on me the two men had anticipated. I became hesitant and awkward. I was going to tell them that both Julio and I had partners, but I began thinking instead of some of my father's more embarrassing diary confessions: his frequent resort to prostitutes throughout his Italian years; his need to have his intense physical urges satisfied before being able to concentrate on 'higher matters'; his naivety and self-delusion in believing that several of the women to whom he turned would have happily slept with him for free.

'We'll try and find you a fifteen-year-old,' announced Diomidio, thinking that this would clinch the matter. He said I was completely wrong to be attracted to women more or less in my age bracket. 'Instead of one forty-five-year-old you could have three fifteen-year-olds,' he argued, bursting into a laugh. 'I make a point of never looking at any woman much over the age of twenty, other of course than my wife. Being with old women makes you feel old. Being with young ones always makes you feel young and fit. The demands of a fifteen-year-old keep you in better shape than any workout at a gym. Take a look at Alfredo. He's in his early fifties. But doesn't he look much younger than his age?' We then learnt the secret of

Alfredo's supposed youthfulness. Alfredo happily told us that he had eight children by five different women, 'each one younger than the last'.

I was relieved to get back outside. So was Julio. We sat down on our usual seats on the gangway and went back to watching what Isherwood had called 'the gradual unwinding of the river and the shores', a spectacle of which we too had yet to tire. The Andes, though visible only as blurred patches of blue, gave us something else to engage our minds, until the next distraction.

We were able to enjoy a peaceful half-hour before the cry of 'Migueleeeto' put us once again on full alert. Diomidio pulled up a chair next to us. His face was unusually serious. I could not imagine what other murky aspects of his sexual life were about to be revealed. But he wanted to tell us about something entirely different, about yet another of the traumatic memories that haunted the *Catalina*'s crew and which were coming to infect our own memories of the journey, even as we absorbed the river's moments of greatest beauty.

The memory of the incident had been triggered off by the village we were passing, 'Regidor, *kilómetro* 429.2', a village outwardly little different from so many other small communities we had seen – humble, precarious-looking, half-obscured by the trees and vegetation along the river's banks. Regidor, according to Diomidio, had been a notorious guerrilla stronghold, a place that always raised a shudder whenever you came near it. Attacks, he said, could happen anywhere along the river, but sailors had always felt more able to relax once Regidor was behind them.

In the 1990s, when the troubles were at their height, Diomidio had worked for one of the coal barges that had been based at Campo Alegre. The worst attack he had ever experienced had taken place just beyond Regidor, when he was beginning to enjoy that feeling of security which always came after passing the village. It was then that he saw a launch advancing towards the barge. At first he thought the three people on board were soldiers coming to check on the cargo. But when they got up to board the barge, he noticed their rubber boots. 'That's always how you can tell the difference between a soldier and a guerrilla. A soldier wears leather boots, a guerrilla always has rubber ones.'

The guerrillas politely explained to Diomidio that they were at war with the Colombian government. They then took control of the barge and forced it nearer to the shore, where Diomidio saw the guns of fifty of their companions pointing towards them. 'What was so frightening was how young the guerrillas all were. They all seemed to be in their teens.'

The three guerrillas on board began placing sticks of dynamite everywhere. 'I asked them what they were doing, and they said they were going to blow up the barge. "Why on earth do you want to do that?" I said. "If you destroy the barge you destroy the livelihood of the poor people you're meant to be supporting." "Your company has not paid off its war debts," they answered. "But what war?" I argued. "Colombia is not at war with anyone."'

Diomidio and his eleven-strong crew were ordered to lie down on their fronts. 'That's it,' he thought, 'I won't be seeing my wife again or my two young daughters. They'll shoot us and then blow us up. Great, what a wonderful way to go. But then something happened to change their minds. Perhaps a call from above. We were all waiting to die, and then they left the boat and took the dynamite with them.'

Diomidio paused for a long while. I was still half-waiting for the big laugh of his that always followed his stories, however unfunny they were. But all that eventually came was a melancholy reflection. 'I've always thought back to what really went through my mind during those moments of waiting for the bullet. And do you know, if I was absolutely honest with you, I don't think I was thinking of anything. My mind went completely dumb.'

He paused again. 'I keep on remembering the incident, just as I keep on remembering seeing my friend the pilot fall overboard and die. I imagine that when I'm old and senile, and my mind is not as it was, they'll be among the last memories to go. Together with my memories of falling in love, of the birth of my children, of the death of my parents ... And, of course, of going when I was young to the Carnival at Barranquilla.'

Clouds loomed over the Andes. The central range had vanished, but we were now travelling parallel to the eastern range and were getting ever closer. The scenery, after its earlier moments of dramatic transition, had settled down to the same dominant elements – the lush green banks, the row of blue mountains behind, the layer of clouds that were engaged in a restless acrobatic display, dispersing and regathering, thinning out and darkening.

The soldiers had begun talking to us. We benefited from our new intimacy to ask one of them for a realistic assessment of the security situation along the Magdalena. He said everything had been reasonably quiet over the past three years, though a soldier from another platoon had recently been killed in a skirmish further up the river. He invited us downstairs to play a coin game with one of his mates and a group of sailors. The lively, explosive atmosphere that ensued made us briefly oblivious of the sweltering heat and noise of the lower deck. We felt more connected with the life of the boat. Our minds were drained of all other thoughts but that of winning. I was cheered when I did.

But I was starting to be concerned about Diomidio. He had come in search of us, and had gone away almost saddened and perhaps even a bit jealous at seeing us happy in the company of others. His solitude was becoming ever more apparent, though not as much as Alfredo's. Ever since we had started eating our suppers on our own, and revealing little more than a polite interest in his doings and musings, Alfredo had become an increasingly spectral presence, a person with a lost and haunted look. The rejection of his and Diomidio's offer to take us to a Gamarra brothel was probably the final blow to his sanity. We returned like good children to our seats on the gangway above. We were keen in any case to get back to the panorama of the Andes, which were now so close to us that we could just about make out their crags and fissures. We had some further moments of pure enjoyment before another sight tarnished the view – a floating corpse, this one larger than the last and carrying with it almost a dozen hysterical vultures. Only when it came to within a few feet of where we were sitting could we finally see what it was – a cow.

Once again Julio had initially mistaken it for a person. He said that his mind had clearly been affected when he was younger by the tales of human corpses floating down Colombia's main rivers. There was apparently one village along the Cauca where an average of around fifty corpses each week were washed up on the shore. He explained that an absurd clause in Colombian law had prevented people from reporting these corpses to the authorities. They had feared they would be arrested as murderers.

Diomidio, who had stood silently behind us when the cow had floated past, now embarked on a morbid monologue, addressed to no one in particular: 'The sights I've seen floating on this river. You wouldn't have believed them. They were worse than those in any horror film. Headless young children. Women with amputated breasts. Eyeless faces. Castrated men. Bodies with all their innards missing. Exposed entrails. Entrails being picked apart by vultures ... They all get to you in the end, these sights. They lodge themselves in your soul.'

I remembered a Bergman film I had seen as an adolescent in London. It had given me nightmares for weeks. It was about a couple who lived on an island in the Baltic archipelago. They were dying from what the leaflet of the Hampstead Everyman Cinema described as cancer of the soul. There was a scene when one of them, or perhaps both of them, tried to get away from the island. My only clear memory of the film is of a small boat being unable to progress any further. The person steering it tries to find out what is wrong. He finds he's got stuck on a seabed of skeletons.

I began imagining the Magdalena as flowing over the remains of all the people who have disappeared into its waters. I wondered how much longer we could continue sailing. Then a rainbow leapt into the deepening blue sky, taking my thoughts elsewhere.

The rainbow was forming a complete half-circle when Julio and I went on our evening stroll, rather earlier than usual. The evening was so exceptionally beautiful that we wanted no one to disturb our enjoyment. The earth beneath the grass and trees of the banks had gone a russet red. Oxen were casting long shadows in the meadows. The profile of the Andes was sharpening against a sky of theatrically lit clouds scattering into puffs of black and white.

I had forgotten to switch off my mobile. My brother had finally reached London and was calling me about my mother's state. She had been eating and drinking so little that she had fainted when he had tried taking her out of bed. The doctor had come again, but had still found nothing wrong with her. She had managed a whole glass of orange juice.

Julio was looking repeatedly towards me, as if willing me to get off the phone. Too polite to say anything he waited for me to stop talking before telling me to rush with him into the enclosure on the last barge. He had noticed that this was where the sailors kept the wooden tripod they took out every evening. He got me to stand on it right next to him, several feet off the ground. 'Cling on tight!' he shouted, his normally unruffled features betraying signs of panic.

I had absolutely no idea what was happening until I saw the barge advancing towards power cables swung across the river. He thought we wouldn't be as lucky as we had been going underneath Barranquilla's Pumarejo Bridge. He was convinced the tanks wouldn't make it this time. He saw them hitting the cables and turning the *Catalina* and its convoy of barges into a live mass of high-voltage electricity. He hoped the wood would be our protection. 'This is it!' he cried, gritting his teeth when we were level with the pylons. The tanks succeeded in getting through, but only just.

The sailor whose duty it was that evening to hang out the lantern was the one whose birthday it was today, Popeye. He was amused when we told him what we had done. But he didn't think we had been wrong to be so cautious. 'You never know with the Naviera Fluvial,' he said. 'I sometimes think they don't have a clue about what they're doing.'

He told us about the rumours of a change of plan for tonight. We perhaps wouldn't be stopping near Gamarra after all, but would simply be jettisoning the tanks there. Julio and I stared at him incredulously, wondering why we had brought the tanks all this way just to leave them in the middle of nowhere.

'After twenty years of working for the company', he continued, 'I've learnt that the only way of surviving is to take everything philosophically and not to question anything. I've thankfully only three more years left with this job. I want to get through them without losing either my life or my sanity.'

*

Of course we'll be staying the night outside Gamarra, declared Diomidio. Julio and I were delighted, though not for the reasons our captain or Alfredo would have wanted. We had plans for visiting a place recommended to me in Barranquilla by the composer Luis Fernando Franco – a club dedicated to the Afro-indigenous music known as Chandé. The idea of briefly exchanging the *Catalina* for an environment manically pounding to the drums of one of Colombia's most exuberantly joyous musical traditions seemed almost too good to be true. And it was.

'I can't let you out on your own in Gamarra,' insisted Diomidio. 'It's far too dangerous. This is not like Barranquilla or Calamar or Yatí. Every place south of Gamarra is dangerous, even the smallest villages. Barrancabermeja is more or less safe by day, if you stick to the centre and don't go to the outlying districts. But if you go out at night, you're taking your life in your hands. Puerto Berrío, where you're thinking of going to afterwards, is one of Colombia's most dangerous towns. It's never safe, not even in the middle of the day, not even in the town square.'

I could see by the look in Julio's eye that he wasn't taking any of this seriously. I, too, found it difficult to believe what Diomidio was saying. What did worry me was his increasingly deranged behaviour. He had still not finished his speech about security. He was getting louder. He was emphasizing his points by constant repetition.

'Up to Gamarra everything is more or less fine, but from Gamarra onwards everything is different. From Gamarra onwards life become dangerous, extremely dangerous. From

Gamarra onwards it's nothing but delinquency, guerrillas and paramilitaries. *Delinquency, guerrillas and paramilitaries!*'

We were almost at Gamarra. It was eight o'clock in the evening and a few lights were glowing along a dark shoreline of palms and a solitary water tower. It did not seem the vibrant, edgy metropolis I had imagined. Julio went off in search of the best viewpoint from which to photograph the town, silhouetted against its fading backcloth of mountains and a deep-pink sky. I remained leaning on the railings of the upper deck, listening to a heated dispute behind me between Diomidio and Alfredo.

I gathered that it was still not certain whether or not we would be stopping for the night. Alfredo was arguing that it would be ridiculous to move on, while Diomidio was saying that he was still awaiting instructions from Hector in Barranquilla. The two men then headed off towards the bridge. Ten minutes later we pulled up at a landing stage just beyond the town. When I next saw Diomidio I asked him to tell me in all honesty what was happening.

He admitted that he didn't really know. It was a Saturday evening and no one was taking his calls at the Naviera Fluvial's office. But he said in a cheery and positive tone that we would probably be continuing that night, and leaving the tanks where we were now, 'Capulco, *kilómetro* 477.7'. The tanks would then be picked up later by a more powerful tug-boat than ours, one that was capable of negotiating another of the difficult stretches of river that lay ahead. 'The good news', he continued, 'is that if we set off tonight without the tanks we'll be in Barrancabermeja in no time, perhaps as soon as the day after tomorrow.'

Alfredo was angry and miserable. He mumbled just a few words as he passed me on the deck. The tanks, he said, were his responsibility. He was the person who had to ensure their safe arrival at Barrancabermeja. If they stayed at Capulco, he would have no other choice but to stay with them, and to camp out beside the quayside with one of the sailors.

By 9.30 Alfredo's fate had been sealed. Sailors were gathering to begin separating the tanks from the rest of our convoy. An hour later we raised anchor and sailed into the night. The sailor who had been chosen to remain with Alfredo was the one who had killed the turtle. He told me before saying goodbye that we would have to eat the animal on another occasion. He promised to freeze it.

Julio and I, and the two soldiers on night duty, were the only people left on deck after the lights of Gamarra had vanished. We were dreaming about the night of music and dancing we could have had. I was also troubled by an alarming possibility. When I had eavesdropped on the conversation between Diomidio and Alfredo, I thought I had heard something about going back in the morning to collect the tanks, 'if necessary'.

Julio was certain I had misheard this. He soon convinced me as well. If there had been the slightest doubt about what to do with the tanks, the only course of action was surely to have waited in Capulco. To sail all night, consume a vast amount of money in petrol, and then return immediately? It didn't make sense. It surely wasn't possible.

'With the Naviera Fluvial, as with fiction, everything is possible,' concluded Juan Cano, producing the line that best summarized our days on the *Catalina*. We had woken up to another memorably clear dawn. The clarity was in contrast to the mood on board. The boat was moving so slowly that it had almost come to a stop. Diomidio rushed past me without his usual greeting. I could hear him shouting on a walkie-talkie. He was trying to get a message through to Hector. He said to the other person on the two-way radio that he had been waiting desperately for instructions since the night before. He couldn't wait any longer. 'When Hector gets round to replying, tell him to call me on the boat's radio. None of our phones have a signal.'

Not even mine. Leiva told me over breakfast that we were sailing through a scarcely populated stretch of the river. And no, he didn't know what was happening. 'No one does.'

Juan Cano, the voice of reason, was fortunately on duty on the bridge. He confirmed to Julio and me what we might otherwise never have believed: that we might indeed be going back to Capulco, to pick up the tanks and then head back again, possibly arriving where we were now in about twenty-four hours' time, 'at the very earliest'. Then Diomidio came in to tell Juan Cano to turn off the engine. He said he wasn't going any further until Hector got back to him.

Without the engine running, the silence was so great that we could hear the cries of the egrets and the lapping of the river's waters. We all sat down outside, under the shadow of the bridge – myself, Julio, Diomidio, Juan Cano and a shaven-headed soldier who looked like the star of a B-movie. As we stretched our feet out on the deck, Diomidio joked that this was just like being on holiday.

Neither Julio nor I was in the mood for talking, nor even for enjoying a swampy, reedy landscape unbroken by mountains. Had we had an infinite amount of time at our disposal we might not have minded the sensation of being stranded in a void, barely contactable by the outside world, not knowing whether we would be going forward or back. But the rainy season would soon be with us, and my mother, for all I knew, might be on the point of death, if not dead already.

Hector's instructions finally came through. We would indeed be returning to Capulco. Julio and I had had enough. We later confessed to each other that, more than anything else, it was the thought of seeing Alfredo again that had determined our decision to escape from the *Catalina* whatever the cost.

Diomidio was clearly not prepared to help us, but Juan Cano was. He said that there was a daily passenger service between Gamarra and Barrancabermeja. It left Gamarra at around six in the morning, and we would probably be passing it in about three hours' time. Our boat's horn would be sounded to wave it down.

After Juan Cano had gone back to the bridge to turn the *Catalina* around, Julio and I went back to our cabin to pack our belongings. Within ten minutes Diomidio was frantically knocking at the door.

He said that as the captain of the *Catalina* it was his duty to look after the safety of his passengers. He realized that we were grown men and knew what we were doing, but he felt he had to make us entirely aware of the extreme danger we were about to let ourselves in for. Everywhere along the river there would be people waiting to pounce on us, or rather on me.

'Remember,' he spelt out slowly and emphatically, 'the first objective of every guerrilla and paramilitary is the gringo!'

He had one more thing to say, a word of practical advice directed to Julio: 'If you do go ahead with your plan, you mustn't under any circumstances allow Miguelito to speak. Do all the negotiations yourself, pretend your friend is from Medellín. That'll explain his strange accent, should anyone ask him any questions.' Then he left.

We had a good laugh afterwards. The idea of my not being taken for a gringo was amusing enough. But the idea that some Colombian, however uneducated, could think that my foreign way of speaking was typical of Medellín was utterly ridiculous.

However, Julio was far more worried than he was letting on. It was part of his character to dissimulate his fears, to appear always calm, sceptical and gently amused. He also didn't want to frighten me; it was part of his role as my unofficial bodyguard. But he now told me something he hadn't told me before: 'When I told my mother I was going to be travelling with this English friend all the way to the Magdalena's source, she immediately went to find out all about you on the internet. "You're going with him, with that old gringo? You must be mad. You'll be kidnapped within days."'

We were trying to decide whether there was the slightest basis to Diomidio's warning when Juan Cano arrived at the cabin. He said he had been let off the bridge for half an hour and wanted to say a proper goodbye, 'just in case we don't have the opportunity to do so later'. We told him about Diomidio's visit, and asked if it really were possible that potential kidnappers would be taking an interest in my movements along the river. 'It's possible,' he admitted, with an expression untempered by its usual underlying irony.

'But you've made absolutely the right decision,' he added. 'Judging by what I've heard about the state of the river ahead it could be ages before we get to Barrancabermeja, even if we weren't losing a day. In any case, nowhere in the world is completely safe today. There's no such thing as risk-free travel. And risks are good for you. There are so many people on this boat who are stuck in their jobs because they are too frightened to look for something else. If you always go for the safe option your life will rush past without you knowing what you've done with it.'

The sound of the boat's horn, overriding the rattle of the engine and the air-conditioning, brought Juan Cano's philosophizing to an abrupt end. Pacho appeared at the door to say that the *chalupa* had already arrived, an hour and a half before we were expecting it.

We crammed our remaining belongings as fast as we could into our rucksacks and hurried out onto the deck. Diomidio and most of the sailors were waiting to see us off. We gave them all cursory hugs and said we hoped one day to see them again, knowing we almost certainly never would. It would have been quite an emotional departure had not other thoughts been preoccupying me. Were we really doing the right thing? Had I left anything behind? How on earth was I going to get into the *chalupa* without falling into the water?

The *chalupa* was like a covered metal coffin, with a long narrow opening through which you had to enter feet first and almost horizontally into a claustrophobic space already crowded with goods and other passengers. The vessel took some time to right itself after I had struggled clumsily into it. Julio managed a more elegant boarding.

My face seemed almost level with the water and my knees were hopelessly trapped near my chin when the *chalupa* roared off upriver, as if trying to break some speed record. The *Catalina* disappeared within seconds. We were moving at a pronounced angle and curving our way around the sandbanks. Should we have hit something and overturned we would all have been trapped under the metal. There were life jackets above us but no one was wearing them. No one had enough space in which to put them on.

I succeeded with a series of contortions to extract my phone from my pocket. It had been ringing again, but had gone dead by the time I was able to answer it. 'Hello, hello!' I shouted in vain, instantly breaking my cover as the man from Medellín. We stopped at a hamlet to pick up two more passengers, and then at another one to leave some sacks of potatoes. I was conscious of people pointing at me from the shore. Or perhaps I was imagining this.

PART THREE
THE DISAPPEARED

10

A giant of a man, with several days' growth of beard and a wave of greying hair, was staring at us from the quay at Barrancabermeja. It was not even midday. Life had been brought forward. The town I thought we would never reach was suddenly here, its massive petrol refinery impinging on the journey like the switching-on of a bright light. I had hardly had the time to think about what we would be doing next. I had spent much of the past three hours dwelling on the advice of some Colombian friends in London. Don't stop long at Barrancabermeja, stop only to change boats, or get on a bus or plane. Better still, don't stop at all. They said it was Colombia's grimmest town. They said that its very name reflected its history of bloodshed: the Red Gully.

The giant was not alone. There were two others with him and they all seemed to be waiting for us. They ignored the other passengers getting out of the *chalupa* and blocked our path to the chaotic taxi rank beyond. 'It was difficult not to spot you,' commented the giant as he introduced himself in a deep, booming voice as Guido Rippamonti, a friend of the composer Luis Fernando Franco. At the mention of this name I instantly relaxed. Help had come our way.

I had met Luis just once, at the Barranquilla Carnival Club, when he had spoken to me about the Magdalena's musical traditions. Yet he had regularly been in touch since, sending me messages about people I should meet along the river, insisting I call him should I ever need advice or run into difficulties. Just before our arrival at Barrancabermeja I had managed to text him a garbled line about what had happened to us.

The remarkable spirit of solidarity that guards the traveller in Colombia had been speedily called into action. Guido, on hearing from Luis, had broken away from a weekly gathering of local intellectuals to come and meet us. He was with his girlfriend Yolanda and a university lecturer who was also a participant of this Sunday meeting or *tertulia*. They were now all going back there, and expected us to go with them. We squeezed into the lecturer's car.

A human warmth engulfed me. It emanated not only from my new companions, but also from the town itself, which was like a smaller version of Barranquilla, a jumble of warehouses, villas, gardens and gaudy shops, run-down, confusing, unattractive, luxuriant, intoxicating, alive. The place filled me with an energy that magically dispersed the uncertainty of the past few days, together with that persistent sense of being on a journey towards some inescapable tragedy. I had been given a reprieve. I wondered how long this would last.

Julio and I were at a critical stage of our journey. We had covered almost 650 kilometres of the Magdalena and were nearing the halfway point. Passenger and cargo boats had once continued a further 200 kilometres to Honda, where the cataracts begin. Our latest information was that today's boats went no further than Puerto Berrío, the next port along from Barrancabermeja. If we were to follow the river to its source, we would have to do so from here onwards mainly by road, track and footpath. We had little way of knowing how long this would take and whether our available time would be sufficient. And there was still the security situation to worry about: though we would soon be out of paramilitary land, we were aiming eventually towards a part of Colombia still troubled by fighting between the Army and guerrillas.

Counteracting all these concerns was a strong feeling of having embarked on a journey that was now unstoppable. The river, with all its beauty, dangers and violent history, was like a drug to which both Julio and I had become addicted. To abandon it at this stage was to risk a profound sense of anticlimax, and to miss out on what could only be an unforgettable finale of tropical mountains and moorlands. The Andean source that lay at the end of all this seemed ever more alluringly mysterious the more I recognized the hardships of getting there. But for the time being, in the car with Guido and his friends, I was barely thinking of the difficulties ahead. I was relishing my new situation, enjoying a breathing-space in the journey, anticipating replenishing my spirits with a pleasant Sunday of socializing. The house to which we were being driven, around the corner from Barrancabermeja's sprawling market, had the name 'El Paraíso' painted outside on the distempered plaster. Its squat, narrow facade fronted what looked like a down-at-heel municipal social club. The other members of the *tertulia* were waiting for us in a large garden at the back, under the shade of a solitary ceiba.

The garden, with its unkempt patch of grass and a tall brick wall overlooked by warehouses, reminded me of a place in industrial Budapest where I used to meet up during the Communist period with a group of dissident cherry-picking intellectuals. The people now greeting us were also reminiscent of my Hungarian friends from the past, a mix of the scruffy and the anachronistically formal, united by a passion for culture and the exchange of ideas.

'Julio, what on earth are you doing here, and with this gringo?' laughed one of them, a wiry man in a string vest who embraced Julio as if they had known each other all their lives. He explained to the rest of the group that they had recently met at a writer's workshop in Bogotá, and that they were mutual friends of the wandering chronicler Cristian Valencia, the discoverer of the Biblioburro. The more I travelled, the smaller the world was beginning to seem. By the end of the day, it would seem smaller still.

We sat down in a circle, like actors coming together for the first rehearsal of a play. Everyone introduced themselves to us and told us what they did. As I listened to Guido, I realized how much the two of us had in common. A North Italian by birth, like I was, he had been brought up in Lombardy, where my mother's ancestors were from. Then he had fallen in love with the Hispanic world. He had moved to Buenos Aires in the early 1990s, and from there had embarked on a slow journey the whole length of the continent, settling nowhere for less than a few months. He and his Mexican companion Yolanda had been in Barrancabermeja for almost three years. They had at last found a place where they felt they could settle for ever.

Yolanda, shyer and much younger than Guido, took over the story. They had got together when Guido had been living in a commune outside Buenos Aires. They were both actors by training. In 1998, equipped with a camper van and a circus-like tent, they had set off on their travels, making a living by teaching theatre to young children and putting on their own performances. Guido, as a good Italian, also had a sideline in food. An expert in the construction of wood ovens, he sold home-made pizzas and gave courses in the making of mozzarella and artisanal beer.

There was a strong idealistic basis to their activities. They believed that experimental theatre, backed by good food and drink, would make the world a better place and lend support to communities traumatized by conflict. In Barrancabermeja they had set up home in the suburb which had suffered a senseless paramilitary massacre in 1998 involving over thirty deaths.

Then the eyes of everyone in the circle were turned on Julio and me. What had brought us here to Barrancabermeja? Where were we going afterwards? There were the usual sighs of envy when I spoke of our Magdalena journey, and smiles when I said that we were like the explorers of the Nile and would not give up until the source was reached. And then Guido asked about our immediate plans.

I tried now to be serious. I talked about my interest in this part of Colombia as the epicentre of Colombia's troubles and how I wanted to learn more about the exceptionally high proportion of its inhabitants who had 'disappeared'. Guido and Yolanda promised to help me in this, but not before tackling an issue of 'far greater importance'. What did we want to do for lunch?

'*Che bello!*', '*Che buono!*' The rapturous exclamations of an Italian friend I had not seen in years came almost to my lips as I sat with Julio, Guido and Yolanda at one of the open-air restaurants that crowded Barrancabermeja's shoreline. We could have been on holiday in the Mediterranean, surrounded by Sunday revellers, eating freshly caught fish, talking excitedly, enjoying new friendships. This joyful scene, coming so soon after our abrupt departure from the *Catalina*, was one I could not quite believe I was witnessing. And its unreality was compounded by a sight I thought I would never see at all – the mythical-seeming *Humberto Muñoz*, now occupying the quayside like a luxury cruise ship in a southern Italian port.

Guido, repeatedly filling our glasses with Chilean wine, was savouring the fish with an infectious enthusiasm, while exchanging gastronomic memories with me, of incomparable dishes of pasta, of the finest seafood, of restaurants where he had eaten 'divinely'. The enchantment of the atmosphere took my mind far away from recent fears and sadness, so that when

I started thinking once more about my mother, I forgot for the moment the ill and frightened old woman she had become and thought of her in the Sicily of her youth, as an actress in a provincial touring company, at the turning-point of her life, on the night when thoughts of the war would be supplanted by a vision of love and future happiness.

Guido, who had begun plying me with questions about my Italian background, shook his head in amazement when I told him of my mother's involvement in the Teatro Sperimentale di Messina. He turned out to have a passionate interest in Italian theatre and cinema of the 1940s and fifties, and had read all he could on the subject. He even claimed to have seen her name in a history of her innovative company, alongside those of such famous actresses as Anna Magnani and Silvana Mangano.

I had to confess that my mother was not in their league. As far as I knew, she had only had two roles of any importance. One was as the barmaid in the first Italian production of J.M. Synge's *Playboy of the Western World*, in which she had been required to use a Sicilian accent. The other was as the messenger in a tragedy by Seneca that included a line so regularly recited by her in later life that it became part of our family lexicon: '*Ecco Roma, ornata di troffei.*' ('Here is Rome, garnished with trophies!')

I had once assumed that my mother was acting the messenger on the night when my father had fallen in love with her. But neither she nor my father ever spoke to me in any detail about an occasion I liked to think of as one of their most ingrained memories. The idea of a grand passion taking root on a provincial stage in wartime Italy had always set my own imagination flying, giving me intensely romantic expectations of love that could never be fulfilled. When eventually I read my father's war memoir, with its account of what he chose to remember of that night and its aftermath, I felt cheated, as if an important part of my life had been based on an illusion. In this account he described with banal matter-of-factness how he went one evening to the theatre and was encouraged by one of the journalists he was with, Franco Libero Belgiorno, to go afterwards to meet the company's director and lead actor, Ennio Cerlesi. Cerlesi introduced them to three other members of the cast. Belgiorno then had the idea of bringing them all back to have supper in my father's apartment.

The actors asked him about the state of English theatre, and enjoyed a meal which 'included items unavailable to Italians at the time'. They stayed until 2 a.m., and were also invited for lunch the next day. My father was particularly taken by one of the two women in the cast, Mariagrazia Paltrinieri. He found her 'lovely looking, very sweet and most intelligent'. That she had been a law student, just like he had, was also in her favour. That she was someone whose obvious joy of life and love of being an actress was belied by what he perceived as a 'very homely personality' ('not quite one's usual idea of an actress') seems finally to have clinched it. He knew there and then that he could be happily married to her. 'As indeed has been so,' he starkly added, as if summing up a legal case. Only after turning to my father's diary, which the memoir so brutally paraphrased and censored, was I able to appreciate what my parents' first encounter must truly have been like. Though his lengthy diary

description of their budding affair lacked the intense romanti-
cism of my imagined version of events (not least for revealing
that the play in which my mother was performing was not a
Seneca tragedy but 'a very light comedy'), it brought their emotions compellingly alive, far more so than the memoir.

Guido urged me to give the full 'uncensored' account of
their story. It had a particular interest for him, as he knew several of its protagonists from his extensive research into this
period. He had read the drama criticism of Belgiorno ('one of
Italy's most famous critics') and was able to confirm the
importance of Cerlesi, who apparently worked also as playwright and film director ('he must have died only two or three
years after your father met him'). He had also seen films star-
ring the two other actors who had come back to my father's
apartment, Gino and Mimosa Baghetti.

I went on to relate some of the more telling details from my
father's diary description of the romance: the rain that had
poured all evening; my father's initial reluctance to go out;
the pushiness of Belgiorno ('a tiny, insignificant-looking but
extraordinarily self-assured man'); my father's previous experience of actors as being 'such terrible poseurs'; his serving at
supper of tins of baked beans and suet pudding; his conclusion
at the end of the meal that he himself was 'far more conti-
nental in character than British', and that the presence of other
British soldiers at the table would have detracted from the
heated excitement of the occasion. 'I feel', he wrote, 'that other
British could not have entered into the lives of those Italians as
I could.'

What the diary evoked so much more effectively than his

memoir was the precariousness of my parents' budding love
for each other. The evening after their meeting in Syracuse, my
mother was moving on to the nearby town of Augusta; and
two days after that, my father was due to be transferred to the
Italian mainland. In his diary my father gloomily reflected on
the 'awful impermanence of one's relationships in the army'.
After periods of 'deep loneliness, longing for a more permanent
relationship with a woman', my father had finally found someone whom he 'would like to see a lot more of' only to be
separated from her almost immediately. 'Heaven knows when
if ever I shall see her again.'

Once more it was Belgiorno who intervened in my father's
life. Persuading him that my mother was as smitten by him as
he was by her, he suggested that my father go and see her the
next day in Augusta and try and bring her back to Syracuse
for the night. Belgiorno had the strong impression that
Mariagrazia was a 'woman who seldom gave herself, but when
she was really attracted to a man, she would'. Not until over
a month later, when stationed in Trieste, did my father write in
his diary the 'long story' of what exactly happened when he
went after my mother, 'a story which I feel sure is going to
affect my whole life'.

I left the tale dangling in mid-air. I had abruptly gone silent, my
mouth half open. Guido and the others were staring at me
expectantly, waiting for me to continue, wondering perhaps if
I had forgotten what I was going to say, or if something were
wrong with me, or if I were displaying the first symptoms of
my parents' illnesses.

I had been distracted by a sudden thought: of the actual sheet of paper on which my father had typed his first impressions of my mother. The page stood out among the others in his diary by being the most worn, dog-eared and heavily scrawled. When I remembered it now, I had a numbingly sad image of my father as an old man, repeatedly turning to this page as he looked back on his life, trying to hold on to what was left of his past. The print, revealingly, had been so continually exposed to the light that it had faded almost to the point of disappearing.

I said nothing more about my father, and the conversation moved on. But as we all clicked our glasses to celebrate our getting together, my mind wandered off again. I wasn't thinking this time of my parents. Guido's promise to talk soon about Barrancabermeja's 'disappeared' turned my thoughts to someone else – to the lost Italian friend whose child-like enthusiasm had been expressed in regular sighs of *'Che bello!'* and *'Che buono!'* His presence somehow lingered among us.

All of a sudden I thought I knew why. I had a strange feeling that this friend, Sandro Trevisanello, had known Guido. He had been in Buenos Aires at the same time. He had worked at a leading pizzeria frequented by the city's Italian community. Eventually I asked Guido.

He put down his glass and stared at me with an expression as disbelieving as mine must have been on spotting the *Humberto Muñoz*. *'Che buono … Che bello!'* he said, perfectly imitating Sandro's way of talking. Sandro, he announced, had been his flatmate in Buenos Aires. Sandro had gone with him to live in the commune. 'And you,' he asked, 'what's your connection to Sandro?'

Sandro, I explained, was someone I had met over thirty-five years ago in the North Italian town of Treviso. We had come to think of ourselves as soul brothers. We were exactly the same age, and shared the same capacity to forget all our worries in the enjoyment of life's simple pleasures, a good meal, friendly company, a beautiful landscape. We had imagined being friends for ever, going together on holidays with the many children we were bound to have, sitting one day as old men on some Mediterranean square. 'Whatever happened to Sandro?' wondered Guido. 'He had such a love of life, and yet nothing ever went well for him. He was always falling in love with beautiful young women. He was the biggest romantic I've ever known. He was continually searching for something he would never find.'

I told Guido that he had married twice but, like me, had never had any children. The last news I had was that he was working in a bus-station cafe near his North Italian birthplace. I had tried to contact him there, but he had already left, no one knew where.

Guido suggested continuing our conversation back in his house, where he said he kept a bottle of reserve grappa for special occasions such as this. But before getting up, he held out his glass to propose a toast.

'To Sandro,' he announced. 'To absent friends. To the disappeared.'

A bridge separated Barrancabermeja from the suburb where Guido and Yolanda lived, the Barrio El Campín, a place which

Diomidio would certainly have advised Julio and I not to visit. The bridge, according to Guido, once had a terrible reputation, as a sort of Bridge of Sighs leading to a suburb where you were likely to be killed or to disappear. 'Even four years ago', he said, 'people thought we were crazy to want to live here. Yet it's one of the friendliest, most trouble-free places we've ever known.' Yolanda nodded in agreement.

The suburb seemed pleasantly green and normal, with simple cubical buildings widely dispersed around a flat, grassy expanse. A teenage band playing harps, drums and flutes marched by us as we climbed the outdoor steps to Guido and Yolanda's second-floor bedsit. The house had several cats and a lame dog, all of whom had been saved by Yolanda from Barrancabermeja's streets. She stroked them as we sat down in a room whose main decoration was a couple of ethnic rugs, a colourful hammock and a banner proclaiming 'The Fight against Forgetting'.

Guido, relaxing in a string vest and pouring us large glasses of grappa, started telling us about the massacre that had taken place in 1998, and about what he and Yolanda were doing to 'ensure that the missing will never be forgotten'. Their initial involvement in the cause was due to the encouragement of a celebrated Jesuit priest, Francisco de Roux, whom they had met shortly after coming to Colombia and who had been their principal mentor and supporter ever since.

De Roux was a exceptionally brave person who had lived in Barrancabermeja throughout the time when the central part of the Magdalena Valley (the Magdalena Medio) was known as the most dangerous region in the world. He had become

Colombia's leading spokesman for the country's voiceless poor, the main sufferers of the country's civil conflict. He was an enormously popular man with an almost saintly fame. 'No guerrilla or paramilitary would dare to attack him,' Guido confidently pronounced. Julio, judging from his expression, was not so sure.

This part of Colombia, Guido reminded me, had been one of the worst affected by the conflict between guerrillas and paramilitaries. The guerrilla movement had been born in the mid-1960s as a result of the continuing failure of Colombia's politicians to protect the rights of the peasantry. The FARC, the largest of the guerrilla groups, had focused its initial attacks on landowners (the biggest of whom came to be the leaders of Colombia's drug cartels), while another group, the ELN, set its sights on destroying the Magdalena Medio's major source of wealth, its petrol industry.

The guerrillas, with their kidnapping, their appropriation of private property, their recruitment of children and their brutal reprisals if anyone disagreed with their views and their methods, became ogres to the majority of Colombians and eventually inspired a violent backlash and the formation of the paramilitary groups. This new movement, originating around Medellín, soon spread into the adjoining Magdalena Medio, where it established its principal stronghold. It flourished thanks to the support not just of landowners, petrol companies and drug barons, but also the Church, the Army, Communist-fearing North Americans and even prominent members of the Colombian government. The former president Álvaro Uribe (whose father had been killed by guerrillas) was famously behind the formation of the citizens' defence group known as CONVIVIR.

The paramilitaries acquired an image as fearful as that of the guerrillas and were responsible for some of Colombia's worst massacres. They were certainly to blame for the one that took place in the Barrio El Campín on 16 May 1998. Forty or so of them turned up that day, at around 9.40 in the evening. They went straight away to the local football pitch, where celebrations and a bazaar were being held in honour of Mother's Day. They killed one youth outright and lopped off the penis of another with a machete. They proceeded into the heart of the barrio, shooting six more people and rounding up twenty-five others. These others were never seen again, nor was anyone ever brought to justice. Someone with considerable power and authority was covering up for the culprits.

Guido and Yolanda had arrived in Barrancabermeja shortly before the tenth anniversary of the massacre, for which an important commemoration was being planned. Yolanda, with the blessing of De Roux, had recorded personal testimonies from friends and family of the victims. These were published in a book to which Guido had given the arty title *To Return Without Having Left*.

I skimmed through a copy as Guido and Yolanda took it in turns to tell me some of the stories she had collected, all of which testified to the complete randomness of the paramilitaries' action. The Barrio El Campín was not a hotbed of revolutionary socialism but an apolitical and predominantly devout neighbourhood, many of whose inhabitants had come here to escape from the disturbances in the countryside. Apart from one solitary old man, quietly watching television when the paramilitaries burst into his room, the victims had all been under the age of twenty-five and enjoying a night out. One of the most poignant tales was of a teenage couple who had recently quarrelled. The boy, trying to make it up to her, took her to the bazaar to have an ice cream. They were both seized.

The greatest anguish suffered by the victims' families was not knowing what exactly had happened to their loved ones. A former paramilitary commander claimed that the twenty-five missing persons were lying in a nearby communal grave, but no one had seriously bothered to look for this. The testimonies in Yolanda's book disturbingly conveyed the emotion of parents waiting every day for news of their children, hoping for them suddenly to appear back on their doorstep. Most parents had resigned themselves to the certainty that they were dead, but there were still some who would never give up waiting.

'There's nothing worse', said Guido, 'than having someone in the family who simply disappears.'

We left Guido and Yolanda just after nightfall, to head back to the hotel they had found for us in the centre of Barran-cabermeja. We had an early start the next day. The latest news from London about my mother had been promising enough to allow me to continue the journey, at least for the time being. There was a *chalupa* leaving for Puerto Berrío at 6.30.

When we got to the centre, neither Julio nor I felt ready yet for our hotel. The streets and squares of the city, even on a

Sunday night, were temptingly lively, with families strolling the streets and filling the rows of outdoor bars and cafes.

As we walked from one crowded square to the next, we both agreed that Barrancabermeja was a far more likeable town than we had expected. But neither of us could imagine doing what Guido and Yolanda had done. The paramilitaries might have lost much of their former authority, but they were still a significant presence in the area and were probably not too keen on our friends' activities.

Yolanda had admitted that in the week following the book's publication her heart had missed a beat every time someone had knocked at the door or passed close by on a motorcycle. Guido, with his hearty laugh, had made light of her fears. He was as much of an optimist as our mutual friend Sandro, as he had gone on to prove by talking about his current project, which was absorbing most of his thoughts and energy.

The project was an arts festival he described as likely to be the most important event in Barrancabermeja's history. It was going to be held in May under a giant tent. Writers and performers from all over Colombia would be taking part, together with spokesmen from the country's leading human rights organizations. He had a vision of the event as a collective catharsis, as an affirmation of human good, as a landmark in the 'fight against forgetting'.

'Lovely people but unrealistic, mad hippies at heart,' concluded Julio as the crowds thinned out and we neared our hotel in the middle of the market area. 'I only hope they don't add one day to the statistics of the missing.'

*

We had checked into the hotel just before lunch and had been warmly welcomed by a friendly young receptionist looking little more than fifteen. She was still there ten hours later, all alone in the cramped lobby, with a shiny gold-threaded shawl draped over her shoulders, despite the humid heat. When we approached her for our keys, we noticed that her face was pale and her hands were shaking.

Julio asked her what was wrong. She said that this was her first time doing night duty. She had never wanted to do this before, but she now had three children to support and had no other choice.

But why was she so frightened? Was this a dangerous area at night? She shook her head. Her fear had nothing to do with the living. She was frightened by the dead, by the darkness. She was frightened of the moment when she would have to switch off the light and confront the spirits. A friend had told her about a religious sect which could help her overcome this fear.

What was this sect? She hesitated. 'It's not Christian,' she muttered, 'it's not Catholic, it's not Jehovah's Witnesses or anything like that.' She didn't know what it was. All she knew was that the sect had offered her as protection a shawl they called 'The Tunic of Divine Light'.

I thought about this afterwards as I curled up in a dark bedroom, aware of the play of shadows on threadbare curtains, of the occasional voice and passing car. The unease that had come over me in waves on board the *Catalina* was returning. I was thinking of the disappeared, of the accumulation of absent presences in my life, of the thousands of missing victims who haunted the Magdalena. And as I pictured the young woman downstairs in her shawl, waiting for the spirits, the disappeared came to seem as palpable as the living, and were all around me now, breathing the stifling air, imploring me never to forget.

11

Down by the port, on the point of boarding the dawn boat to Puerto Berrío, I talked with Julio about talismans and religion. I showed him the passport-sized photo I always carried with me of the Santo Custodio, the saintly faith-healer and guardian angel of my adopted Spanish village of Frailes. I said I was not a conventionally religious person. I had inherited lapsed Catholicism from my mother and humanism from my father. Yet I half-believed in the Santo Custodio and in his miraculous powers of protection. I saw him as a supernatural force of good.

The *chalupa*, crowded at first, slowly began to empty as we stopped off at one hamlet after another and the colours of the day brightened and began to glow. I was soon once again in the thrall of the Magdalena, and feeling strangely immune to the precariousness of *chalupas*, even as ours swerved at violent

angles to avoid sandbanks and driftwood. Travelling nearly at
the level of the water brought me into a new intimacy with the
river, which I stared at now with enamoured eyes, experiencing
a sensual thrill at the sight of the bordering meadows, ceibas
and forested promontories.

Julio and I followed our progress on Diomidio's list of
places, as we crossed from bank to bank, pulling up at hamlets with such fantastical names as Witches, Mosquito Net,
Soap Dish, Deer, The Horse, Whale and Masked Man. These
were places where yesterday in the tugboat I might have
imagined delinquents and terrorists spying on us from behind
the trees and the thatch-covered huts. In my current,
dreamier state of mind, they were hugely enticing, inspiring
longings of one day making a more leisurely river journey,
stopping off each night at hamlets such as these, sleeping in
hammocks, eating around an open fire, listening to songs and
stories.

The sentimental, nostalgic mood now affecting me had
much to do with the knowledge that this would be our last
morning sailing up the Magdalena. The boatman had confirmed that there were indeed no more river services after
Puerto Berrío, which we were expected to reach as early as
nine in the morning. I almost wished we could have taken for
ever.

Puerto Berrío approached rapidly to our right, backed by an
ironwork road bridge whose construction in the 1960s had
symbolized the changing face of Colombian transport: the
expansion of the country's road network and the decline of

Magdalena's river traffic. Since then Puerto Berrío had been virtually abandoned as a port.

The town centre, even from the boat, appeared almost untouched since the days of the *David Arango*, unwashed and unrestored. Closer still it could have been a film set from the 1930s, a decayed complex of art nouveau and art deco buildings that might have served originally as small hotels, gambling dens, brothels or the headquarters of now-defunct trading companies. The town, with its former railway link with Medellín, had once been one of the most thriving along the Magdalena.

A small, noisy group of people crowded onto a landing stage guarded by soldiers. One of the soldiers asked to see my passport, while another looked through every pocket of my rucksack. Puerto Berrío, I had been warned, was a centre of the drug trade, as well as a place with strong links to paramilitary groups such as the cheerily named Death to Kidnappers.

A smiling young woman came to our rescue us as we stood waiting and vulnerable in the midst of potential prostitutes, wallet-snatchers, dealers and kidnapper-killers. We had got in touch with her through Facebook. Anticipating a menacing scene on arrival, Julio had sent a message the night before asking if there was anyone in Puerto Berrío prepared to look after our luggage while we walked around the town. Within twenty minutes a woman called Adriana had replied. She was a friend of a friend of his, and worked as a local journalist.

She apologized for being late. Petite, fresh-faced and full of

energy, she looked out of place in the rough, worn surroundings. She took us with our luggage to an office couched
behind the giant columns of a Fifties shopping arcade on the
main square. She then asked if there was anything we wanted
to see during our brief visit to her town. Our first wish was
to have some breakfast. She came with us to what she
described as a 'legendary breakfast establishment', a place
whose dark, ornate facade hid a smoky interior of greasy
lime-green walls.

I told Adriana over breakfast that there were two monuments in particular I was keen to visit. One was the former
Hotel Magdalena, once a luxury hotel equalled in Colombia
only by the Hotel El Prado in Barranquilla. The other was the
cemetery. Adriana smiled. She said she only had time to take
us to the former. She added that we wouldn't be able to visit
it without her. In the 1980s, she explained, during the worst
period of the troubles, it had been turned into an army barracks. But fortunately she was on friendly terms with the
commander.

She rang him to arrange a visit for us all at ten. Just before
leaving the cafe Julio enquired about the security situation in
Puerto Berrío. Adriana, an ostensibly easy-going and open
person, became tongue-tied and nervous. She muttered that
she would rather talk about this outside. Once there she
referred obliquely to two men who had been sitting at a
nearby table. She was worried they might have been eaves-
dropping on our conversation. There were still 'many people
of their kind in the town' and these people continued to hold
a lot of power. She murmured that they were dangerous. One

of her colleagues had received a recent threat. She never spec-
ified who these people were, she knew we would understand.

She was smiling and vivacious again as we set off towards
the barracks. She even joked about her momentary secretive-
ness. But her response to Julio's question had been unsettling.
I had never encountered such paranoia before in Colombia. I
had experienced it in Communist Europe, where friends had
often talked to me only after making sure there was no one
else around and no hidden microphone.

I tried not to make too much of it. The sun was shining
brightly. The street we were walking up was flanked by intact
rows of 1930s houses and shops. The Hotel Magdalena,
crowning a green escarpment, was a cheerful, neo-rococo con-
fection in pinks, ochres and yellows. It conjured up an earlier
and more carefree period in Puerto Berrío's history.

The story of the Hotel Magdalena, said the soldier who was
our guide, was the story of the town. The hotel, dating back to
the arrival of the railway in the 1870s, was given its present
form after 1922, when Puerto Berrío began to experience a
comparatively brief but intense golden age. The building,
though traditional in style, was endowed with all the latest
technology of the time, and has even been claimed as the first
important construction in Colombia in reinforced concrete.
Then, as with the town itself, it slowly lost its lustre, and was
in an uncared-for state by the time the Army moved in.

When I commented on how bright and glowing it now
appeared, the soldier proudly revealed that it was the first
important building in Puerto Berrío to have been restored. He

thought this highly appropriate. 'Now that Puerto Barrío seems at last on the way to recovery, it's only right that we take care of its heritage.' Colombia, he continued, was no longer the volatile place it had been in the 1980s or 1990s, 'or even five or six years ago'. 'We have a few problems with drugs and delinquents, but so does every town in the world.' 'And the paramilitaries?', asked Julio, boldly using the word that Adriana had taken great care to avoid. 'As you know',' smiled the soldier, 'they were demobilized under the presidency of Uribe.'

The soldier, a courteous and well-read young man with a great enthusiasm for history, was noticeably more relaxed when talking about Puerto Berrío's past than its present. As he showed us the many old photos that had been hung in the lovingly restored dining-room, he spoke of all the celebrated Colombians who had eaten there, including the assassinated politician Jorge Eliécer Gaitán. He also talked of the fame of the hotel's balls and parties, and of the many now-forgotten names who had performed at these occasions, the Black Stars, the Hispanos, the Lucho Bermúdez Orchestra, the singer Matilde Díaz.

The imagined sound of their music was with us as he led us through the rest of the building, across the palm-studded courtyard and up to an open gallery, from where an exterior staircase swept down with rococo abandon to a garden stretching almost all the way to the Magdalena. The soldier was telling us about the hotel's popularity with honeymoon couples as Adriana posed in a 1940s armchair. She chatted to the soldier, while Julio went off to photograph an elderly gardener watering a hanging basket of flowers. I poked my head through an open door to discover a reconstruction of one of the original bedrooms.

I stepped sheepishly inside, to study the double bed more closely. I gently fingered its embroidered cotton sheets and felt the pillows for softness. The lithograph above the headstand of a Raphael Virgin was something I remembered from Italian hotel rooms of my early childhood, rooms like the ones my parents had known all over Italy during the war, rooms like the ones in which they had finally come together as a couple.

I had begun prying into a world I would once never have dared to enter. I came from a family where no one ever talked about their emotions or gave anything away about their personal lives. My father's diaries had helped me over this barrier of discretion. Thanks to them I had an intimate knowledge of that aspect of my parents' past that perhaps mattered most – their developing love for each other.

I knew, for instance, that my father had done exactly as his perceptive friend Belgiorno had recommended. Though, by his own confession, he was someone who never liked rushing things, he phoned my mother the morning after she had arrived in Augusta to propose having supper that night once the play was over. She accepted, and he was even able to persuade her afterwards to come back with him in a taxi to Syracuse.

But then, in the taxi, my mother began to worry. She confessed that she had never given in to a man before and that men physically repelled her. She wanted to go back to Augusta;

but she ended up in my father's apartment, she in his bed, my father on the living-room floor. This was my father's last night in Sicily. His main cause for hope was the sense of something deeply spiritual tying them together. And though they had parted 'in quite a formal manner', he had managed to give her the first kiss she claimed ever to have enjoyed.

The exchange of passionate letters began a couple of weeks later, when they were at opposite ends of Italy. They were finally able to see each other again in July, when my father was given leave to travel from Trieste to Rome. There were some awkward initial moments, and my father did not find my mother quite as beautiful as he remembered. But the bond between them strengthened all the same. They would there-after try and meet up whenever they possibly could, no matter the practical difficulties, no matter where.

A different Mariagrazia to the one I had known as my mother seems to have emerged during their long period of courtship. Her almost inhuman degree of self-control was set aside as she became determined to hold on to the one man she had ever loved, the person who – as she once hurtfully told me – would always take precedence even over her two sons. A few weeks after my father's visit to Rome, she set off on the long and arduous journey to the Croatian port of Pola, not even knowing whether she would get there before he had left, and in fact almost failing to coincide with him after her ferry from Chioggia had been held up for a week by bad weather.

By the end of 1944 my father was writing in his diary that his original instinct about my mother had been right: they were a couple who perfectly complemented each other, they had so much in common, they shared so many interests, the same tastes in literature, the same sense of humour, the same views about other people. At the very end of his life, she would be the only person whom he still faintly recognized. His memories of their love would be the only ones he had left, perhaps the only ones he felt worth keeping.

Guido phoned to say that a woman called Pilar would be waiting for us at twelve in front of the cathedral. He said we would learn a lot from meeting her. She was one of the founders of the human rights organization known as Ave Fénix. She would be happy to take us to the cemetery.

We searched the park in front of the cathedral for someone we had imagined as youngish and full of idealistic fervour, someone like Yolanda. In the end Pilar was the one who found us. We hadn't noticed her. She was indistinguishable from the other middle-aged and elderly women who were sitting on concrete benches, chattering away, feeding the birds, lost in thought.

She introduced herself after we had been walking for a while in circles. She had a tightly curled crop of dyed, orange-brown hair, a pinched face and a frail body. She had an expression both forceful and kindly, and the manner of someone who had greatly suffered. She didn't waste time with small talk.

Sitting down with us on one of the benches, she spoke in a low voice about the situation in Puerto Berrío today. I had to concentrate to hear her. Sometimes I couldn't believe I had heard her correctly. Puerto Berrío, she repeated, hadn't

changed all that much in recent years. The people she referred
to as 'they' or 'them' were as brazen and unchallenged as they
had been in the past. They had demobilized in return for con-
cessions that made many of them immune from prosecution
for their past crimes. And still they persisted with their former
terror tactics. One person a day was assassinated in Puerto
Berrío, a town with a population of 27,000. Around the end
of October, during the build-up to All Souls' Day, this figure
rose to three a day.

She pre-empted our next questions. 'They don't necessarily
kill at night,' she said, 'nor in the poorer barrios, nor even sur-
reptitiously. They kill whenever they want, and wherever. They
could easily kill somebody in this square, and in the middle of
the day. And they kill not just over drugs. Often no one knows
why they kill. And no one ever will know, because the authorities have no interest in catching them. A couple of teenagers
from my barrio shot down a neighbour's son just the other
day. He was buying some cigarettes from a kiosk. We all know
who the killers are and where they live. They haven't gone into
hiding. There's no need.'

She told us that Ave Fénix had been founded in 2007 to
break the silence that had surrounded the atrocities of the
recent past. Eight hundred and thirty relatives of the murdered
and the missing had joined up, mostly women whose loss of a
husband left them unable to support their families. The aims
of the organization were to battle for financial compensation
and to keep the memory of the victims alive. 'We receive no
public or private funding. We haven't even an office.'

She got up to take us to the cemetery, where she said we

would see her organization's memorial mural to the victims. We walked for fifteen minutes along a straight, treeless avenue lined with ever more scattered rows of villas. I studied each passing motorcyclist carefully. I wondered how much of a target Pilar was.

My original interest in visiting the cemetery seemed now almost frivolously folkloric. A young writer friend from Bogotá had sent me an article he'd written about a local belief involving the unclaimed corpses retrieved from the river, all of whom were automatically assumed to have been guerrillas. It was said that if you adopted one of these corpses you would be guaranteed good luck and prosperity, with the proviso that a man could only adopt a female corpse, and vice versa.

One day the corpse of a particularly beautiful young woman turned up in the mortuary of Puerto Berrío. She was eventually adopted by a local decorator, who gave her the name of Sonia. The decorator went every day to the cemetery to spend an hour in front of her coffin. During one of his 'conversations' with her, she whispered to him what turned out to be a winning lottery number.

Pilar said that there were fifty corpses of this kind, all of which were contained in a wall of niches behind the cemetery's military mausoleum. We took our time getting there – Pilar had so much else to tell us about, even before entering the main entrance gate, with its flanking plaster walls painted with what was described above as 'The Mural of Memory'.

To the right of the gate, and partly obscured by a vendor and his parasol, was an illusionistic scroll containing the names of 'The Disappeared'. To the left, in full sunlight, was a list of 'The Murdered'. Pilar, stopping in front of the latter to point out the names of her parents and two of her brothers, emphasized that her family had no involvement whatsoever with politics or drugs, nor any reason for attracting attention. 'At least not after 1979, when guerrillas expropriated a small property of my father's in the country. After that we had nothing.'

Her eldest brother was the first to be murdered, in 1987, probably by paramilitaries. The next year her mother was killed, 'no one knows by whom'. The following year guerrillas assassinated her father. Then there was a gap until 1995, when her second brother drunkenly entered a bar frequented by paramilitaries, who shot him and a couple of his companions. 'He might have asked them about the fate of my father's property, which seems to have been seized from the guerillas by paramilitaries. But we don't know.'

No culprit was found for any of the murders, nor was there an obvious reason for any of them. The authorities made no attempt to solve the crimes, and never asked, 'not even once', if Pilar's family had any enemies. The authorities never did anything, not even when a friend of hers was raped by known paramilitaries and went on to develop AIDS.

The first tomb we came to was of a particularly notorious victim of injustice, a promising nineteen-year-old medical student from Medellín. His only crime was to have courted a woman in whom 'one of them' was also interested. He was snatched from his home, tortured and castrated. 'The screams were heard everywhere, but no one did anything about them.' On his tomb his family had written: 'Let God be your companion until we have fought for justice and are reunited beside you.'

Rows of plants and tombs sloped gently up to a crowning group of mausoleums and piled-high niches. Pilar showed us the space reserved for the 'adopted' corpses, the names of whom were scrawled on the plaster like amateurish graffiti. She talked for a while about the ritualistic and esoteric aspects of the three-day celebrations surrounding All Souls' Day, which included a day when flower-covered boats went out onto the river in a symbolical search for the missing, and 'The Day of Memory', when all the tombs were lit with candles. A statue of the Angel of Silence, normally motionless above the cemetery's upper wall, was said to come alive on All Souls' Day itself and to wander down to the medical student's tomb.

But the tale that most detained us in the cemetery was a tale about the living, a tale about 'them'. Julio was as incredulous as I was when Pilar told us that the money earmarked for the victims' families ended up instead with the families of the victimizers. After the demobilization of the paramilitaries, former members of these armed groups were given their own office to deal with requests for compensation from the families of dead colleagues. The story got worse. Pilar had documents to show that when these families received the money, other paramilitaries then went round to demand their share of it. Julio said he was learning something new every day about his country. Pilar made a terser comment. 'Evil', she said, 'knows no boundaries.'

On our return to the town centre Pilar had a drink with us at an outdoor bar. There was a noticeable silence when Julio asked her about the politics of Puerto Berrío's mayor. She said this wasn't a good place to talk. We gathered from her response that he too was 'one of them'. Adriana later confirmed our suspicions after we had gone to her office to collect our luggage. She muttered that the mayor was 'an evil man, a very evil man'.

The buses out of Puerto Berrío left from the main square. Julio and I would briefly be going our separate ways. Now that we could no longer travel by boat, I had decided to make a detour to nearby Medellín, to find out more about the strange phenomenon of memory loss in that area. Julio said that if I didn't mind he would go instead and stay with some good friends who lived in the opposite direction from Puerto Berrío, in the province of Santander. We arranged to meet up here again in three days' time and follow as far as possible the river's banks by bus, first to Honda and then on to the southern town of Neiva and up into the Andes.

My bus came first. The stories we had heard from Pilar had provoked a sudden surge of insecurity at being on my own again. Julio told me not to worry. I still had my Spanish protector, the Santo Custodio, to look after me.

As the bus left the last of the outskirts, I thought again about the cemetery. I was curiously haunted by the image of the vendor who had set up his stall in front of the entrance. As my eyes closed I pictured him under the shade of a tree, an open parasol projecting from his modest table of goods. He was slumped on the seat of a tricycle, his head rolling above an ice box filled with soft drinks. The fringe of the parasol almost completely hid the painted inscription on the wall behind, 'THE DISAPPEARED'.

12

My father was such an absent-minded person that it was difficult at first to tell when his mind began to fade. I suppose the first signs came in his writing and conversation, his gradually narrowing vocabulary, his continual repetition of the words 'cope' and 'iniquitous', his tedious dwelling on the subject of 'traffic' and on how much worse the traffic situation had recently become in London.

I would later learn from my reading about Alzheimer's that he probably already had MCI, or Mild Cognitive Impairment, in his late sixties. He began to show more worrying symptoms around the time of my brother's wedding in Ireland, to which he carried a sheet of paper listing the main people he would meet there and their connection to the family.

I tried persuading myself at first that his new oddness had a rational explanation. I attributed his behaviour at the wedding to his emotion at seeing one of his sons getting married at last. I said to myself that his increased inability to find the right words was part of the normal ageing process. I interpreted his ever more frequent puzzlement merely as a development of his habitual pensiveness.

But after a while my mother and I acknowledged that there was something wrong with him. After one of his oldest friends had come to supper and he had had to ask afterwards who this person was, my mother took him for tests at a local 'Memory Clinic'. The brain scan that was recommended revealed that he had been affected by a series of mild strokes.

In a sense this news was reassuring to my mother. She believed that by keeping his blood pressure down and reducing his intake of salt he would be prevented from having more strokes and would not lose any more of his memory. She also agreed to his participating in a test trial of a new wonder drug that was predicted to halt the progression of memory loss, and even recover some of the memory that was already gone.

His condition gradually worsened, despite the drug, the daily half-aspirin with each meal, the reduced salt and the regular tablets of Echinacea, which a homeopathic friend had always sworn by. My mother now placed responsibility for my father's illness on the fact that his parents had been first cousins. Fortunately, she added, the possibility of any genetic defect being passed on to my brother and I was hugely diminished by her own remarkably healthy family background. 'No one in my family has ever been mad,' she would repeatedly remind us.

Despite his growing forgetfulness, my father was still able to maintain a semblance of normality until his early seventies. Though his progressive inability to judge distances prevented him from driving any more, he otherwise kept to the regular activities he had followed since retiring – writing in the morning, walking on Hampstead Heath in the afternoon, reading in the evening. In contrast to what would happen to my mother, his impaired mind seemed to bring out all the more attractive aspects of his personality, above all his gentleness.

I became closer to him now than I had ever been as a child. Physically undemonstrative towards me in the past, he now started greeting me with kisses and hugs. For the first time ever he invited me to his club in the centre of London, the subscription to which he was about to let fall. This turned out to be the first and last time we would go anywhere together on our own. The momentousness of the occasion was not marked by any revelations in the conversation, though he stirred my curiosity by presenting me with an envelope he insisted I should not open until after his death. Afterwards, seeing him distractedly confronting the traffic of Piccadilly Circus, I felt an overwhelming protectiveness towards him. I realized how easy it would be for him to be run over or lose his way.

Only a few months after the visit to the club he was picked up lost, a few streets away from his house. He persisted in going on his afternoon walks, but my mother was unable to relax until he was safely home. After losing himself a few more times, my mother turned for help to his doctor, who suggested having Care in the Community collect him for daily activities with other elderly people. My father never took to this scheme. He was depressed by the other people. He found them old, decrepit and boring.

His decline thereafter was frighteningly rapid. Looking one day at an animated cartoon with my six-year-old niece, he said how surprised he was to find out that animals could speak. His own power of speech was becoming increasingly limited. Though he always had with him a piece of paper with useful words and phrases, he would eventually communicate with little more than sighs, smiles and repeated utterances of the word 'cope'.

In May 1997, after waking up one evening in his usual armchair, an unread book in his hand, he made out of the blue the last coherent comment I would ever hear from him. He wondered about the existence of 'an upper part', and about whether he would find his parents there. 'I would so love to see them again,' he quietly murmured, before falling asleep again.

In October of that year, my mother put him in a home. The place, specializing in people with Alzheimer's and dementia, was conveniently near to their house. It was also grim, dark and ugly. The nurses did little for their patients other than sit them all day in front of a television set.

My mother, whose emotions were outwardly confined to crying while reading a novel, convinced herself that her action had been the right one. But her stoicism must have hid the most unbearable suffering and guilt. For the first two days after my father's departure, she was advised by the home's director not to visit him. The hope was that this would allow him to acclimatize more quickly to his new surroundings. However, his immediate reaction on seeing her again two days later was to put on his scarf and coat. He was desperate to get out. He hadn't grasped that the home, with its permanently locked front door, was his prison for life.

He didn't live much longer. Whenever I was in London I used to see him at the home every Sunday afternoon. Any evidence of his being able to recognize me soon went. I would sit for an hour or two holding his wrist. He would look surprised and then smile. I wondered what if anything was going on in his head as he sat in the communal sitting-room, surrounded by the groans and banter of the fellow demented, watching uncomprehendingly whatever was on the television but without being focused on anything. The emptiness of his stare was something I would never forget.

The memory of that stare had brought me now to Medellín. I had been here once before, shortly after the city had shaken off its image as a lawless gangland capital to become a showpiece of the new Colombia. I remembered a vibrant modern metropolis, lushly set in a green mountain valley, with a climate always described as that of perpetual spring. This time I was only passing through, hoping for some new insight, however tiny, into my parents' illnesses.

My first priority was to see Doctor Francisco Lopera, one of the world's great experts on Alzheimer's. Everyone in Colombia seemed connected with him in some way, though he proved difficult to get hold of at first. In the end a last-minute meeting with him was arranged by my much-respected host in Medellín,

the writer Hector Abad Faciolince. Hector's father had been an
inspiration to Lopera, as to so many others in the city's medical
community.

Hector, an avuncular man with a cheery Santa Claus look,
had written about his father in a best-selling memoir translated
into English as *Oblivion*. This exceptionally moving testimony
of filial love was the tale of an apolitical, community-minded
doctor who had ended up assassinated by paramilitaries. The
father had earned a reputation as a dangerous communist
simply through his 'desire to leave the world a slightly better
place'.

Unknown to me up till now, Hector was also the author of
a recent article entitled '*El pueblo del Alzhéimer*', which dealt
with the proliferation of the disease in a district a hundred kilometres north of Medellín. Though he had only travelled as far
as the district capital of Yarumal ('a cold and ugly mining
town'), he had wanted to reach the village beyond this,
Angostura, which was said to be where the disease had origi-
nated in the area. However, he had run out of time. He was also
with his new young partner, who had been so depressed by
what she had seen in Yarumal that she couldn't wait to leave.

Angostura, I told Hector, was where I intended going after
meeting Dr Lopera. He told me to be careful, as this village
had a history of guerrillas. He advised me to stay the night in
Yarumal and only visit Angostura in the company of others. A
mutual journalist friend of ours, on a hiking tour of the area
in 1998, had apparently been kept hostage near the village for
several months. 'Of course, that was many years ago, and
nothing is going to happen to you today. But it's best to take

precautions.' He immediately tried to find someone prepared
to spend the next two days driving me around the area. After
a few calls he gave up.

I wasn't as worried as I might have been several weeks earlier. I was becoming more hardened to the warnings I was
receiving in Colombia. They seemed mainly to reflect the
touching concern shown by Colombians towards their visitors.
Colombia, like my London borough of Hackney, clearly had
its dangers, but I had yet to hear of any recent kidnappings or
politically motivated murders involving foreign tourists.

Hector's apartment had in any case a calming effect, and
reinforced the sensation I'd had ever since arriving that afternoon at Medellín: of returning to normality after what Julio
had called some of the 'maddest days' in his travelling life. The
apartment, brilliantly light and tastefully modern, was in an
area of luxury residential blocks and conurbations that clung
to the city's bosky north-eastern slopes. From the large balcony, the city appeared in all its tourist-brochure beauty.

I didn't have as long as I would have liked to enjoy this.
Hector reminded me of the appointment he had made for me
that evening with Doctor Lopera. I couldn't be late. The doctor
was an exceptionally busy man who had found for me some
few spare moments at the end of his working day. I was back
in a world where time mattered more than it had done on the
almost wilfully unhurried *Catalina*. The sky, moreover, was
darkening with clouds. The rainy season, too, was back.

The rain poured without stopping all the way to a clinic at the
other end of Medellín. Even the few yards between the taxi

and the clinic's heavy wooden door were enough to drench me. I was early. I slowly dried off as I waited alone in a panelled room redolent of the 1950s. Doctor's waiting-rooms always frightened me. The thunderclaps outside made this one worse.

Doctor Lopera showed a hobbling woman with a drooping head to the door. Then he came for me. He did not have the look of Boris Karloff, nor of an impatient man anxious to return as soon as he could to important matters. Instead he had the manner of my late Uncle Brendan, that of a doctor willing to spend as long as it took to calm a patient.

His large head, with its thick mass of wavy white hair, nodded sympathetically while I briefly explained my family interest in Alzheimer's, and how an encounter with Gabriel García Márquez had inspired my present journey. He asked me how I had found the great writer. I said that in many ways his mind had seemed as alert as ever.

Then Doctor Lopera talked about *One Hundred Years of Solitude* and about the illness that had affected Macondo. 'What García Márquez described was not Alzheimer's in its usual form, but rather a degenerative disease of the brain that begins with an inability to sleep.' Curiously, he added, several years after García Márquez had written the book, a rare strain of dementia was encountered with exactly the same characteristics.

Yet there was also something Macondo-like about the 'plague of Alzheimer's' that had broken out in the Yarumal district. Before getting on to the subject that had made his name as a scientist, he drew a diagram to illustrate Alzheimer's in general, and its five principal stages, beginning with asymptomatic MCI and ending with the point when the brain fails to send signals to the body and shrinks to up to a third of its original size.

Noticing perhaps my discomfort, he reassured me by saying that having two parents with severe memory loss did not necessarily mean that I would develop mainstream Alzheimer's myself. No one yet knew what caused it, other than just bad luck.

However, this was not the case with what he called the '*paisa* mutation', a reference to the inhabitants of the central cordillera of the Andes. This form of Alzheimer's was an early-onset one whose symptoms were generally apparent by the age of forty-seven. It was a purely genetic disorder caused by changes to 'chromosome 14'. Since the late 1980s, when this strain of the illness was officially recognized in the area, twenty-five families had been identified with it, all of whom were probably descended from a single Basque who had settled in Angostura around 1750. 'These families, amounting today to around five thousand members, constitute the world's largest pool of potential Alzheimer's sufferers. About half of these people could end up developing the disease.' The *paisa* mutation, he continued, was of huge significance for the study of Alzheimer's and the ways of ameliorating it. Thanks to a greater understanding of the illness, care of patients within families was already greatly improving. He also reckoned that in five years' time drugs would be available to hold back the illness's final stages. His own team at Medellín University was concentrating on the early stages, when sufferers were still able to do some light work. Studies of social, environmental and pre-existing medical factors showed that most of these people were from humble, poorly educated agricultural families, and that depression could be one of the disease's possible triggers.

Sitting back in his chair, he asked me if I was thinking of going to the Yarumal district. When I said that I was he repeated Hector's advice about Angostura, and told me about the time when he had had to accompany a reporter from the *New York Times* and a team from the BBC to the village. He confessed that he had been worried about taking gringos there and, as a precaution, had given the villagers no advance warning of the visit. He had also ensured that their stay in Angostura was kept to the absolute minimum.

After a brief pause he wondered what I was doing the next day. He said he was unable to go with me to Angostura, but that he was driving early in the morning to Yarumal, where he was expected at an 'Alzheimer's workshop'. At least one member from the affected families at Angostura would be taking part. If I wanted to come along, I needed to be outside his clinic by 4.30. He warned me that Yarumal was indeed cold and ugly, and had extremely steep streets.

Dr Lopera picked me up at the appointed time. The rain had stopped, but there were no stars in the sky. I had slept for less than three hours. I could hardly keep awake, yet felt obliged to do so. Dr Lopera had promised to make use of the journey by continuing yesterday's conversation. As he drove out of Medellín he started telling me how he had come to discover the *paisa* mutation.

The story went back to 1986, when a farm labourer was

brought to him from the village of Belmira, very near to where he himself had been brought up. This person had begun rapidly losing his memory and his use of words from the age of forty-five. He was now forty-nine and had lost everything. Capable of expressing emotions only through outbursts of laughter and sighing, he had no control over his clumsy movements and had a vacant, undirected look 'as if staring at infinity'.

Various relatives of his were revealed as having suffered similarly, which the family explained in terms of witchcraft and an ancestral curse. The person was taken in for tests, but then released after a few days with the diagnosis of pre-senile dementia. Dr Lopera was struck by how alike this case was to one analysed by Alois Alzheimer in 1906.

Over the next few years, during Dr Lopera's travels through his native district, he came across other such cases, which led him to suspect a genetic strain of Alzheimer's that was widespread in the area. However, a definitive diagnosis of Alzheimer's can only be made after analysing a person's brain after death, something obviously requiring the close collaboration of a family. In 1995 a breakthrough was made when the precociously diseased brain of one of Dr Lopera's patients was presented to Medellín University, thus providing the basis of Colombia's first 'Brain Bank'.

The defective gene was identified, after which Dr Lopera and his team embarked on what amounted to a detective hunt in search of carriers and their genealogical history. Extensive searches were made in parish archives, while reports of potential sufferers were investigated. Perhaps the most useful and enthusiastic helper of all was the team's driver in Yarumal, who would excitedly ring up Dr Lopera with the news that he had 'found another one!'

Inevitably, given the poor rural settings in which these researches were being carried out, the team regularly came across local superstitions, such as the kind that had surrounded the 1986 patient. Other people said that the disease was caused by the excessive use of aluminium in cooking, and some even claimed that the mind was affected when you touched the bark of a rare local tree. A favourite story of Dr Lopera's blamed it on a village priest who had put a curse on his parishioners for stealing from the collections box.

'And the robber of memories?' I sheepishly asked. That, he replied with a smile, was just the invention of a Medellín journalist with a poetic imagination. But what about the legend of the robber on horseback? He said he hadn't heard of it, but that it sounded like a version of one of the bogeyman tales told throughout the world to misbehaving children.

He changed the subject to a more serious problem for those doing rural research on Alzheimer's in the 1990s: the heavy guerrilla presence in the area. An uncle of Dr Lopera's had ignored all advice and bought an isolated estate near Yarumal. He believed that you could negotiate rationally with the guerrillas, who were normal, sensible human beings. They kidnapped him all the same, and asked for a large ransom, which the family had difficulty in paying. When they got their money they killed him, probably because he knew his captors from before or had seen their commander.

One of Dr Lopera's assistants, a Spanish woman, was also

taken, but she was released after only a week. Her story had impressed the *New York Times* reporter, who wrote about how her captors had got back in touch with her several months later, when she was in Medellín. They were keen for her to come and see them. The mother of one of them had succumbed to the memory disease and was urgently in need of help.

Dawn was finally breaking to reveal a scene gloomily appropriate to tales of kidnappings and lost minds. Below the grey, low-lying clouds was an almost Central European landscape of cows, sodden fields and sinuous borders of pines and eucalyptuses disappearing into fog. The cold and damp hit us as we went to have breakfast at a roadside restaurant frequented by *paisa* cowboys with broad-brimmed leather hats and horses tethered outside. There were glimmers of sunlight as we returned, revived, to the car. We talked again about Alzheimer's.

A simple blood test, observed Dr Lopera, can now determine whether someone has the abnormality that causes the disease. This information is always withheld from the volunteers, one of whom told him that he would kill himself should he ever find out. 'Ironically,' noted the doctor, 'this person had already begun to lose his faculties.'

And do many Alzheimer's patients kill themselves as a result of their illness? 'I don't know of a single person who has done so here,' he answered. 'One of the features of the disease is anosognosia – a lack of awareness about what is wrong with you. People always talk about the distress sufferers feel at the onset of Alzheimer's, but the sufferers themselves are probably not aware of anything.' Remembering my father's perennially anguished look in later years, I only hoped that Dr Lopera was right.

The workshop took place in a school just below the town centre. Dr Lopera gave the inaugural power-point presentation, in which he discussed the various types of dementia and stated that there were 36 million Alzheimer's patients in the world. During the mid-morning break he introduced me to a middle-aged woman from Angostura whose father had died of Alzheimer's and whose two siblings also had the disease. She said I shouldn't leave the district without visiting her village, a beautiful place with so much to offer alongside its terrible history.

I didn't return to the late-morning session. The sun was now fully out, transforming Yarumal's cold mountain setting into a picture of tropical lushness. I was impatient to see the town, and keener than ever to find a way to reach Angostura. I called Yarumal's unofficial historian, Mauricio Restrepo, whom Hector had said was a person who could be counted upon to arrange anything.

We met outside the Town Hall. I would not have taken him for a local historian. Young, tall and handsome, with a fashionable haircut and a T-shirt covered in lettering and silver stars, he looked more like a rock star than a deskbound scholar and functionary with a love of provincial life. His first suggestion was that we climb up to the Town Hall's balcony, to view a steeply inclined and unexpectedly appealing main square topped by a cathedral-like parish church. The square was lined with neat rows of taxis and motorcycles, with the odd horse and cowboy to remind you of the proximity of the traditional rural world.

Yarumal appeared so much cheerier than how I had imagined 'El pueblo del Alzhéimer'. 'People have recently been coming to Yarumal expecting the place to be just like Macondo, with everyone suffering from memory loss,' smiled Mauricio. 'But the number of afflicted is minuscule in relation to the rest of the town's population.'

Serious, kindly and energetic, Mauricio had a passion for his native district that soon dispersed all my negative preconceptions. As we discussed what we could do for the rest of the day, we were joined by a like-minded and vivacious contemporary of his, Gloria Gómez, the local health councillor, another rejuvenating spirit. They were full of plans for me, the main one being an outing together to Angostura, a place they made sound like a tripper's paradise.

From the corner of my eye I saw two men following us at a distance of about twenty metres. When we boarded the cramped public van that was headed to Angostura, they got in at the back.

The animated banter between Mauricio, Gloria and me, and the scenery that progressively opened up with each turn of the narrow road, helped me forget their presence, and indeed almost everything else, even the underlying reason impelling me towards the regional cradle of Alzheimer's.

There were ever higher distant mountains, verges sprinkled with flowers, steeply inclined fields, cows grazing under palms, Hansel-and-Gretel-like houses with wooden porches in primary greens and reds. At the entrance to Angostura was a huge, hand-painted billboard promoting the place as the village of a miracle-working priest called Don Marianito. The cobbled square where we alighted seemed to have been conjured up by a writer of children's tales, with its ring of candyfloss-coloured houses, its sparkling green mountains behind, its donkeys laden with sacks, its customized village bus with the hand-painted image of Don Marianito floating in a Hindu-like sea of ornament.

The two men from Yarumal turned to face me. They said they had better present themselves before I got 'the wrong idea'. They had come to Angostura for my 'security and peace of mind'. They were secret police.

They kept a discreet distance as I was guided around the village by Mauricio and Gloria, who acted as if the encounter with my mysteriously appointed bodyguards had not taken place. I was taken into the church and then into an adjoining house to see clothing that had belonged to the locally born Don Marianito, currently in the process of being canonized. I was shown split sacks of drying coffee beans, outlying banana plantations and a main street with a lingering colonial air.

Gloria mentioned taking me to a household afflicted by Alzheimer's, of which there were ten in Angostura alone. Sightseeing the ill didn't appeal for the time being and I opted instead to spend our remaining hours in Angostura enjoying a leisurely lunch in a restaurant named after Don Marianito. Even the policemen made no further show of being on duty, and came to eat with us under the pergola of a colonial courtyard, at a long table on which there gradually appeared all the great gastronomic treats of the area: drinks made from maize, cheese-flavoured flatbreads, chorizo, goat stew, sugar cane wrapped in banana leaves.

'Eating', commented Gloria, towards the end of the copious lunch, 'is often the last pleasure of the Alzheimer's patient.' The clouds were returning. I remembered how much my father had enjoyed his food, and how he had kept his appetite until only a few days before his death.

The sky was completely overcast, and a hailstorm imminent. We were back again in Yarumal, having fondly said goodbye to our police escort. We had been talking and laughing right up to now, but had become respectfully silent as we stood outside a house at the very bottom of a nearly vertical street. Gloria knocked on the door.

Hector had been to this house, as had every journalist with an interest in Alzheimer's who had come here. The place seemed to have turned into Yarumal's Bedlam, a place that lured visitors with a morbid curiosity in the mentally abnormal. I was reluctant to go there, even just to talk to the family's two remaining healthy members. I felt awkward, voyeuristic and nervous.

But Gloria said that the mother and daughter who looked after their family loved having people come to see them. They needed distractions, they needed constant encouragement in their thankless task as carers. And they clearly loved Gloria. The warmth with which the mother greeted her at the door made me slightly more comfortable about our visit.

The mother, with her black clothes and long grey hair

carelessly tied back in a bun, looked straight out of a Greek tragedy. The daughter, a former nurse, was a short, mousy woman with bags under her eyes and an overall look of exhaustion. We sat in their sitting-room, listening to them talk about the mounting difficulties of their situation. The mother's husband had died of Alzheimer's at the age of seventy-two, a good ten years after showing the first symptoms. He had been the lucky one. Four of their thirteen children had developed the disease in their early forties. One of them, also a sufferer from Parkinson's, was being looked after in Medellín. The other three were living in the house with their mother and one of their unaffected sisters.

Gloria explained to me that hardly any of the afflicted families in the area would dream of leaving their relatives in a care home. The one Alzheimer's patient who had been placed in care at Yarumal was by far the worst-off of her fellow sufferers. She had been virtually abandoned by her family, and was completely isolated from the other inmates. She only smiled today when food was given to her.

To be cared for lovingly by your family, continued Gloria, was by far the best solution, at least for the patients. She turned to our two hosts and said with a warm smile that you had to have the patience of a saint and the constitution of an ox to be such wonderful carers as they were. 'You have to give up almost everything, even your sleep.'

Gloria was someone who appeared unfailingly positive about life, and to have the ability to transmit this feeling to others. However, not even her happiness and optimism alleviated the horror of what we saw next.

She had gone on ahead, with our two hosts. Mauricio and I had been left alone in the sitting-room, relieved that we had got away with just a polite conversation with two dedicated carers. But the mother returned to tell us to follow her, to a suite of darkened rooms at the back of the house.

A man in his early forties, with nothing ostensibly wrong with him, spoke to us at great speed about wanting to go out. 'My youngest son,' murmured the mother, as we continued towards the bedrooms, the doors of which had been taken off so that the patients could always be in sight. 'He was only diagnosed a year ago.'

I almost closed my eyes on being shown into the first bedroom, where a woman, not even in her fifties, lay propped up on her side, motionless apart from some twitches of the head, her large teeth exposed, her eyes wide open, her expression like that of someone trapped in an unending nightmare. I moved on quickly into the adjoining room, where I sensed immediately what I had felt on entering my father's bedroom the morning of his death. A sudden chill. A momentary certainty that there was absolutely nothing at the end of life, that an 'upper part' did not exist.

'He could stay a few more years like this,' said the mother as we paused in a front of a man six years younger than I was but looking already like a corpse, utterly grey, his drawn face protected from the light of a curtainless window by an open umbrella. 'He's still remarkably strong, he sometimes has violent movements that are difficult to restrain.'

His brain, like those of his siblings, would probably finish up in the Neurosciences Department of Medellín University, labelled as another example of the E280a or *paisa* mutation, analysed for the build-up of plaques, and for what Dr Lopera had defined as 'the substitution of alanine for glutamic acid in codon 280 of the presnile 1 gene on chromosome 14'.

What I wanted to be told was what science could never tell me: what, if anything, had stayed in his mind? I needed reassurance. I needed to believe that certain thoughts and memories would always remain, strong enough to counteract any sense of emptiness ahead, to invest life with its transcendental moments as you continued travelling upriver, towards an enigmatic source.

13

Mountain walls in patchy dark green came right up to a Magdalena that was altogether different from the river of before, far narrower, and far faster. I was seeing it in frustrating snatches from the bus to Honda, sitting once again with Julio, planning our journey's final stages.

We worked out that in as little as two days' time we could be at the ancient Andean settlement of San Agustín, the nearest we could get to the source by bus. The main and overriding uncertainty was the stretch of mountainous jungle between San Agustín and the source itself. We had yet to meet anyone else who had done this.

Most travellers journeying up the Magdalena had got little further than where we were now. Boat passengers catching a train to Bogotá got off at Puerto Salgar, while others sailed on a few more kilometres to Honda, a once-thriving trading centre controlling the traffic between Bogotá, Medellín and the coast. We were staying the night in one of the old-fashioned, resort-like hotels that dotted Honda's outskirts.

The weekenders and Colombian holiday-makers had all left the town. The owner of the almost empty restaurant where we went for our off-season supper closed early in order to guide us on a moonlit tour of the old centre, with its columned neo-classical market hall, steep cobbled alleys and deserted streets shadowed by wooden porticoes. We imagined ourselves in a colonial ghost town, surrounded by the spirits of the Magdalena's past.

Though we were now in a hurry to continue southwards, we fitted in an early-morning visit to the nearby town of Mariquita, where we spent a frustrating hour searching by taxi for places associated with the botanist José Celestino Mutis. Mutis had been based here in the 1780s while organizing his exhaustive surveys of the Magdalena. He had also created a legendary garden here later to be recreated in Madrid's Botanical Gardens as a showpiece of the Enlightenment.

Mutis was one of the reasons I had first become interested in the Magdalena, but traces of his presence in sprawling Mariquita were difficult to find. We were directed three times to a humble suburb named after him, before arriving by chance at an austere, long-fronted colonial building that had been the headquarters of the Royal Botanical Expedition. We were told that the young man with the key had had a dental emergency. He eventually turned up to show us a scattering of engravings and a small reconstruction of Mutis's original garden, dominated by a few bamboos and ceibas.

The pathos of history hit me afterwards as I paused beside a simple stone church that stood ruinous and alone in the town's threadbare old centre. Adjoining its padlocked front door was an arched opening protected by chicken wire. I peered inside to see a bearded soldier in sixteenth-century armour lying recumbent at the corner of a cloister, his face and legs crudely painted the colour of flesh, his eyes highlighted in blue. An inscription identified him as the heroic Spanish conquistador Jiménez de Quesada, the founder of Bogotá, one of the most illustrious figures in Colombia's history. Bankrupt, disgraced and suffering from leprosy, he had come to die in 1574 near the point where the Magdalena's waters had 'born down with such force that we could proceed no more'.

As I slumbered on the Neiva bus, I was brought to life by a familiar voice calling me on my mobile. 'Migueleeeto!' shouted Diomidio. 'Are you still alive? You should have stayed with us, we're having fun.' I asked where they were. 'We're about fifty kilometres south of Gamarra, we've been stuck here almost since you left. And where are you?' I said that we had just entered the province of Huila. Over the crackling of the fading line I heard him warning me again about guerrillas. Julio, drowsy with sleep, chuckled as I told him all this.

The Magdalena Valley broadened once more into a flat agricultural expanse extending to the provincial capital of Neiva, our final stop before the Andes. We were offered floor space by a friend of Julio's who lectured in English at the local university. His cramped bachelor's house was at the end of an anarchic row of small residences, somewhere towards the edge of the town's suffocating, centre-less maze. He was a lover of books, and had an extensive collection of them, each of which was wrapped up in plastic as 'a protection against wood-worm'.

He said how much he enjoyed the life of Neiva, 'a very quiet town except when the terrorists decide to make themselves heard'. Huila was in a part of Colombia still referred to as a 'hot zone', and Neiva itself had suffered a number of bomb attacks in the past. 'But the town has been calm for years,' he quickly added. And San Agustín? He said that he had heard of no recent reports of guerrilla attacks in the area, but we should be on our guard when changing buses at Pitalito, 'a lawless town controlled by drug bands'.

He changed the subject, proposing a night out dancing by the Magdalena's banks. We went with two of his female students to an elegant outdoor club stranded in a riverside wasteland where he advised us not to wander. There were fairy lights hung from the trees, coloured lanterns on the tables and cushioned wickerwork seating that seemed almost suspended above the loudly gushing river. The waiter brought us a bottle of rum as we tried to talk over the competing sounds of the cumbia and the Magdalena. When Julio and the others escaped onto the dance floor, I stayed behind for a while, mes-merized by the violence of a river swollen by storms further up the valley.

We went back to the friend's house at around two in the morning and were sitting outside at the front when the street's jovial night-watchman dropped by on his bicycle for a swig of our rum. He was persuaded to show us his machete, which he swished around karate-like in the air before posing menacingly for a photo. In my dreams that night the glint of flashing steel merged into a memory of waters churning in the darkness.

The Magdalena had turned into a mountain torrent. We were ascending rapidly from Neiva, climbing ever higher above the river's narrowing valley, looking down upon a Magdalena that had become an angry slash across a vast and daunting landscape. The air was cooling, and rain clouds had begun forming over the tropical peaks ahead.

By late afternoon we were already at Pitalito. Even though we had no intention of going anywhere beyond the quiet, outlying bus station, Julio's lecturer friend had 'taken the precaution' of getting a former pupil of his to meet us on arrival. The pupil, now actively engaged in local politics, was with two colleagues, one of whom was a former mayor, the other the person in charge of tourism for the area. They were going to drive us to neighbouring San Agustín.

They laughed in the car when we told them about the lecturer's portrayal of their town as a place where even sitting outside at a bar during the day was a risky activity. 'He should get out here more often,' said the pupil, whose two colleagues confirmed that Pitalito was now as safe and quiet as San Agustín, and that the area's image had so drastically improved of late that foreign tour groups were an ever more frequent sight.

I told them that we were intending to reach the Magdalena's source in the Páramo de Las Papas, but still did not know how we would get there. The composer Luis Fernando Franco, who

had been so reassuring about every other aspect of our journey, had done his best to dissuade me from visiting the place:
he claimed that it was a good three or four days' ride from San
Agustín, and in the middle of a zone of continued fighting
between guerrillas and the Army. Other reports suggested that
the source was now easily accessible by Land Rover.

'You certainly can't get there by car,' said the pupil. 'But I've
heard it's a manageable hike from the town.' His colleagues
agreed with him, though they hadn't been there either.

They stopped the car at the start of the drive's final climb,
so that we could photograph the Magdalena as a distant,
diminutive ribbon of cataracts hemmed in by steep slopes of
scarred green. Then we continued under a slight drizzle to San
Agustín, a town of dirty white walls and dark tiled roofs
spreading out over a rounded landscape of fields, woods and
faraway valleys. Among the first people we saw on the damp
high street was a blonde-haired family with baggy patchwork
cardigans.

The town had famously been a magnate for hippies, who
loved the softness of the climate and scenery, the mystery of
the archaeological remains, the excellence of the cannabis, and
a special hallucinogenic mushroom unique to the area. The
pupil reckoned that there were now about twenty foreigners
living in the area, 'mostly entrepreneurs clever enough to
exploit the place's enormous tourist potential before too many
Colombians get in on the act'.

I sheepishly admitted that the place where we had planned
to stay was run by a Swiss man known to friends of mine in
Bogotá. Everyone in the car was perplexed at first when I

mentioned its name, then one of them nodded and smiled. He said that it had an eccentric reputation.

A young man on a motorcycle was waiting for us at the entrance to a muddy path, a few kilometres outside the town. With his wavy long black hair, goatee beard and large innocent eyes, he looked like the protagonist of some Romantic drama by Schiller. He spoke with barely a trace of accent, and had hispanized his name to Felipe. He rested one of our rucksacks on his handlebars and swung the other one onto his back, and then drove off. We had been instructed to walk in a more or less straight line for about twenty minutes.

The mud was so deep in parts that it came almost up to our knees. But we could happily have put up with anything for the sheer pleasure of being in open countryside and stretching our legs after so much recent confinement in boats and buses. The walk was also a beautiful one, across fields that rolled gently down towards what appeared to be the edge of a deep valley.

Felipe was lying with our luggage in the thick grass surrounding a couple of round huts roofed in bamboo. He unlocked the door to one of them to reveal an incongruously immaculate ochre-painted room with an undulant, abstract mosaic that turned out to have been the work of his ex-wife, a Bogotá designer.

We caught up with him again further down the hill, at one of the humble farm buildings that formed the nucleus of his Finca Hostal La Chaquira, a place whose advertised attractions and facilities included hiking, horse-riding, visits to the Magdalena Gorge, tranquillity and 'living with nature'. Felipe himself lived alone in a dark, ascetic structure with Tibetan prayer rolls and dozens of kittens and puppies. I got the impression that he had few people coming to stay, and was not trying too hard to attract them. He said he preferred word-of-mouth publicity, so as to get the sort of clients he liked, 'relaxed and open-minded'.

The focal-point of his modest Hostal was a thatched-roof pavilion, with a long wooden table at which, he said, all meals were served, prepared by himself. This is where we now sat down to ask him about the Páramo de Las Papas. I had begun to wonder if anyone actually went there. But he revealed that he had recently returned from a camping tour of the area, accompanied by one of San Agustín's 'best and most reliable guides'. He had wanted to do the trip for years.

'Tourists', he added, 'are frightened of visiting the Páramo. It's a long way away. The conditions are tough. The path through the jungle is steep, narrow and slippery. And it's still thought of as FARC territory, even though the Army today keeps strict control over the area.'

He said he hadn't seen any guerrillas during the time he was there, but seemed impatient to move on from the subject of security. Instead, he wanted to tell us why we should visit the Páramo at all costs. With an almost idealistic fervour he went on to say exactly what I wanted to hear: that the beauty of the moorland was not quite of this world; that reaching the source was a near-spiritual moment.

The intense look in his eyes, as of someone who had recently undergone a life-changing experience, made me believe him. He had stirred both my excitement and my fears.

The chosen goal of my journey seemed even more haunting and challenging than I had expected. Felipe, getting down to the practical details of our trip, said we could save time by taking a public van to a village called Quinchana, from where it was just a two-day ride to the source. He offered to organize this for us and get hold of the guide he had mentioned. He said we should be able to set off the day after tomorrow, having whetted our appetites beforehand by a visit to the area's main archaeological sites, and to a famous beauty spot, a few kilometres outside San Agustín, where the Magdalena is squeezed by rocks into a gorge less than a metre wide.

The storm we had been anticipating came to nothing, and a faint sun appeared towards the end of the afternoon. Felipe thought we had time before supper to walk to the site after which his Hostal was named, La Chaquira. I was already impatient to see some of the megalithic carved stones for which the area was famous.

The track we had taken earlier descended to a rocky outcrop high above the deep, winding valley created by the Magdalena. The rocks were covered in carvings, some of which were very worn, but not the principal one – a large, stylized figure with outstretched arms and a disproportionately sized head whose giant eyes seemed to be staring out across the valley. They would have seen a cascade shooting hundreds of metres from a gully on the opposite side, beyond which were distant wooded mountains fading into the clouds.

This was archaeology how I selfishly, romantically liked it: out of the way, neglected, in harmony with nature. The intensity of the silence, though eventually broken by the huffing of a group of elderly German tourists, was conducive to meditation. It made me reflect on the sacredness of the carvings and on whether their specific placing in the landscape had a hidden significance.

The remarkable civilization that had produced these works, between the first and eighth centuries AD, had remained unseen by westerners until 1753. A Franciscan friar, travelling in that year between Bogotá and Quito, came across dozens of megalithic sculptures in what are now the outskirts of San Agustín. He didn't know what to make of them. Some of them looked to him like grotesque parodies of Christian monks and priests, but this was rationally impossible: their workmanship clearly predated by several centuries the arrival of Christianity to the New World. His only conclusion was that they must be the work of the Devil.

Ever since I had first become fascinated with South America I had wanted to see San Agustín's famous 'archaeological park'. When conceiving my Magdalena journey, I had thought of the park as one of the main rewards for travelling to the river's uppermost reaches. On my first morning at La Chaquira, setting off with Julio towards the San Agustín road, I wondered how much the enigma of the carvings and their creators was related to the mystery I perceived at the Magdalena's source.

A taxi-driver friend of Felipe's picked us up at the end of the track. He told us that we would not be disappointed with the park, it was one of the wonders of the world. His way of talking, different to that of someone from the coast, had an authentic ring about it: it was discreet and carefully considered, and with a faint hint of the proverbial Andean melancholy. He appeared so trustworthy that we contracted him for the rest of the day. His name was José. He said that in his life as a driver he had known many bad people, but that he had recognized our goodness from the moment he saw us.

José drove us to the park's main entrance, where Agustín's leafy suburbs peter out into a landscape like that of a tropical Ireland fringed by distant high mountains. Coachloads of schoolchildren, dutifully learning about their national roots, barred our progress forward, but were soon lost in the vastness of the site. We descended in hushed reverence into the dark 'Wood of Statues', where individual monoliths were tidily displayed amidst the dense fauna, like points of interest along a nature trail.

I searched for meanings in this mass of sculptures that united so powerfully the abstract and the figurative, the stylized and the eerily naturalistic. 'I wonder what these dudes were smoking when they carved this shit,' exclaimed a solitary backpacker who tagged along with us through this hallucinatory world of suns, moons, phalluses, birth-giving women, eagles clawing snakes, twinned bodies with a single head and men in tall hats brandishing what looked like cricket bats.

Everything was somehow connected with death and the afterlife, the main part of the site being arranged around four burial mounds guarded by clusters of these strange figures. Most intriguing of all, and acting perhaps as a symbolic focus to all this, was a stream whose exposed bedrock had been hewn into what was both a monumental work of sculpture and a testimony to the hydraulic skills of the San Agustinians. Faded reliefs of animals (iguanas, toads, salamanders, chameleons, lizards, snakes, turtles with human heads) surrounded a maze of intertwined channels and basins through which water from a nearby spring flowed effortlessly and without spilling.

The carved bedrock, believed today to have been a place for religious ceremonies and ritual baths, was evidence perhaps of what I had hoped to find – a river cult fomented by proximity to the Magdalena's source, the spring of memory, the fountainhead of creation, the entrance to the underworld. But as I looked for clues in this watery labyrinth, aspects of the modern archaeological park began increasingly to irritate and distract: the adjoining cafe and visitors' centre, the bland landscaping, the pagoda-like roofs above the monoliths, the protective metal-and-glass structure that prevented any close look at the bedrock carvings. The demands of modern tourism and archaeology began to seem like a harness keeping in check elemental forces that had so obviously disturbed and puzzled the Franciscan visitor of 1753.

'So what did you think?' asked José on collecting us at the park shortly before lunchtime. 'Extraordinary,' I enthused, keeping to myself the feeling that three hours of walking around the site had been as much as I could take. I was now readier than ever to embark on the final stage of the journey, to head off the beaten track, to glimpse a virgin nature.

José, thinking of ways we could happily spend the rest of

this day of waiting, proposed a long lunch at a village restaurant on the other side of the valley to Felipe's property. On the way there we would have to make the sharp descent to the especially narrow stretch of river known as the Magdalena Gorge.

A couple of souvenir stalls marked this popular beauty spot, alongside a panel whose words '*Viva El Magdalena!*' were as rousing and invigorating as the sight of the river below, gushing between walls of rock. But as we edged our way down to the water's edge, we were reminded even here of death's stalking presence. A young couple, very much in love, lay passionately kissing under the shadow of a black cross ringed with floral tributes.

The restaurant to which José took us specialized in guinea pig, the most famous of Andean dishes. A battery farm, crammed full of these rodents, stood at the back of the pleasant beer garden where we awaited our food. The restaurant's owner said that guinea pigs were very shy animals, and only liked being touched when someone knew how to do this properly. He held in his hand the petrified creature he was about to kill. Its grilled innards were served first, as an appetizer accompanied by popcorn. We were also offered a glass of its blood, which was said to taste like red wine.

The rest of the animal came with our main course, by which time the conversation had got on to the inescapable subject of the troubles. Obliquely referring to the guerrilla group known as the FARC, José told us that 'they' had made this village virtually out of bounds to outsiders and for many years the restaurant had been forced to stay closed. The situation, he added, had been no better in San Agustín, which for a long while had also been under strict guerrilla control. The FARC had instigated what he called 'a reign of terror' in the area.

Any illusions I might have had that being under the vigilance of the FARC was a softer option than being under that of the paramilitaries were now challenged by José. Though he sympathized with their aims of helping the rural poor in their battle against exploitative landowners and politicians, he said he would never forgive them for the sufferings they had caused 'the innocent'.

The curfew the guerrillas had imposed in San Agustín was an example of their cruel intransigence. For a few years it was impossible to go out in the town at night, even if you were driving someone to hospital. An acquaintance of José's had been turned back by guerrillas when taking his pregnant daughter for an emergency operation. Others like him had been shot dead on the spot.

Then there were all the children who had been recruited by the FARC, many of them young boys who had been tempted by the promise of guns and the thought of becoming a real-life B-movie hero. Still more had been taken forcibly from their homes and told to forget their families, and that the only family that mattered was the FARC, a family you could only leave in a wheelchair or a coffin. Those who tried to get back to their real homes seriously endangered the lives of their relatives and were ruthlessly hunted down, even if they were hiding away in the middle of a large city.

José, apologizing for talking too much, said nothing more about the FARC. 'The worst times seem fortunately over,' he murmured, looking down at the table. The restaurant's owner had reappeared and was giving him a stare.

Everything was set up for our trip the next day to the Páramo, Felipe reported on our return that evening to his Hostal. Another guest had unexpectedly arrived, a serious young computer engineer from Stuttgart, travelling with a guitar. Speaking to us in broken Spanish he expressed his view that the FARC was treated unjustifiably badly by the press. According to him, they were fighting a legitimate battle against a corrupt government. Neither Julio nor I was lending him our full attention. We were more concerned by the spiders that kept on falling onto the table from the roof. 'They're harmless,' assured Felipe, 'they're just baby tarantulas.'

Felipe was delighted to have secured us the guide he particularly liked, a man known to everyone by his nickname of Torito. 'There are other guides I don't trust nearly so much,' he added, mentioning in particular a person known as Gallo, a deeply disturbed person who had once made a lot of money as a *huaquero*, a robber of tombs. For Felipe that was the worse crime possible, and one which always carried a curse. There was apparently an ancient tomb on his property, but he had refused to dig it up. 'I don't like disturbing the spirits of the dead.'

Though the guinea pig had taken away my appetite and Julio's, Felipe insisted on giving us a lavish supper in preparation for the days ahead. He returned two hours later with a large dish of *rösti* and San Agustín's 'finest sausages'. He had also managed to get hold of several bottles of Chilean wine and some 'high-quality cannabis'.

He gave us a final briefing about our trip. Torito's sole fault, he said, was that he talked too much, and often didn't let you quietly enjoy the landscape. 'Be very firm with him from the start and tell him you enjoy silence.' The only other thing we had to worry about was the weather. The conditions were often so terrible that the landscape could be completely hidden.

I didn't sleep so well that night. I woke up after an hour, with the rain battering against the roof, heightening my gloomier imaginings. I was worried not just about the weather but about everything. I was a nervous and almost wholly inexperienced rider. I was frightened about encounters with the FARC. I did not want the enchanted journey from Barranquilla to end as a dangerous uphill slog leading only into clouds. I was terrified that this was what old age would be like: growing difficulties, a persistent fear, an ultimate nothingness.

But then, falling in and out of sleep, the rains cleared in my dreams, the colours returned to the mountains, and I was tracing the great river of García Márquez's childhood to its origins, excitedly anticipating a time when I would be able to tell the writer about my journey, about how the magic of the Magdalena had remained undiminished to the very end, about how, on the eve of riding to the source, I had thought again of the colonel facing the firing squad, remembering the day when his father had taken him to discover ice.

We got up at 4.30 in the morning to walk in total darkness towards the road. The rain had stopped, but storms throughout the night had made the mud on the track worse than ever.

José was on time to take us into San Agustín for our dawn meeting with Torito. He envied us our visit to the Páramo, about whose beauty he had heard so much. He had an intuition that we were going to be lucky and that the sun would light up the Magdalena's source for us. He and his wife had been praying all night for our safety and well-being. He said once again that we were 'good people'. He made us feel as if we were innocents, in need of protection, on the point of stumbling into a world we would never fully understand.

14

As we started off that day towards the Magdalena's source, towards that place of legendary beauty, I had a glimpse of myself as a young student entering the Warburg Institute for the first time, looking up to see the name Mnemosyne, and reading afterwards that she awaited travellers at the entrance to the Underworld, where she guarded a spring alongside that of Lethe, the Goddess of Forgetting.

And then I was in the darkness of a pre-dawn San Agustín, meeting up with our guide Torito. He was a wiry, weathered figure with a large moustache, a yellow sweatshirt and a white baseball cap. His looks and funny nickname betrayed his Caribbean origins, which Felipe had told us about. But he did not seem at first sight to be the proverbially sunny Caribbean type, nor the lovable, loquacious joker whom Felipe had described. He appeared taciturn, nervous and shifty.

He began to smile more once he had been paid his advance and we had all got into the open red van that was taking us to the village of Quinchana, at the start of our horse trek. During our thirty-five-kilometre journey there, which took almost two hours, we heard snatches of Torito's life. He had been born in a suburb of Cartagena. He had moved to the Andes when he was a young man. He had lived in Quinchana for twenty-five years, but had recently moved back to San Agustín.

The ride was punctuated by stops to pick up children going off to the village school. Torito went to stand on the narrow platform at the back. He held on tightly to the rails of the roof rack, as the surface of the road progressively disintegrated. At every stop he swivelled his face inside the van to give us a goofy grin and ask if we were alright.

There were breaks in the dawn sky as the wooded land-scape opened up and the waterlogged track emerged hundreds of metres above the Magdalena. As the van jolted its way around the contours of a sheer slope, I experienced moments of panic like those I had had along the more terrifying Andean roads in Bolivia and Peru. But the sun was soon out, and we were down by an attractive village almost at the water's edge. We were at Quinchana.

We had made excellent progress, according to Torito, who said that the horses had yet to arrive – a son of his would be bringing them. We waited for them outside the village store, a whitewashed building with large eaves and a painted wooden balcony, like a welcoming Basque farmhouse. Torito became almost endearing as he sat down with us on a bench to talk about his love of nature and animals and how he could never live again in a city. His current project and dream was to buy a farm near Quinchana and turn it into a horse-riding centre for tourists. Felipe had promised to be his backer.

While Torito went off on some errands, several of the villagers came up to greet us, all of whom hoped we would enjoy our stay in the area, and made enthusiastic murmurs when we mentioned that we were heading to the Magdalena's source. Julio asked one old man the inevitable question about security. 'It's been very quiet here recently,' he smiled, 'very quiet.'

Torito had ordered some breakfast for us at the store, where he also suggested we prepare ourselves for the marshes of the moorland by acquiring some tall rubber boots. We decided to buy some beer as well, but the storekeeper said that this was a dry village and it was forbidden to sell alcohol here. Neither of us had come across such a place before in Colombia, but before giving this more thought we heard some shouts outside. Torito's son had turned up with the horses and had started screaming abuse at his father. He had disappeared on seeing us. Torito just smiled and asked if we were ready to leave.

Something was not being told to us, something which fleetingly suggested that Quinchana was a place of secrets. The village's perplexing alcohol-free status and the son's mysterious outburst distracted me for a few moments, until my nerves about mounting the horse and my haste to get going overcame every other concern.

Torito made some last-minute adjustments to our saddles as we waited to depart. As someone who had hardly ridden before I was given the smallest and apparently most reliable of the horses, an ugly, blotchily grey mare known as Pavo or

'Turkey' because of her colouring. Despite her unimpressive size, I almost fell forward over her neck on my first attempt to mount her. Julio, a natural rider, rode confidently behind me on the fearsome steed Satanas, while Torito led the way on his mare Capricho, the appropriateness of whose name we would soon discover.

A flimsy, undulant bridge roofed with sheets of corrugated iron spanned the Magdalena on the outskirts of the village, after which a broad, well-graded track began a sharp ascent through farmland and woods. I had so little initial control over the horse that Torito had to tie her to his. But gradually, as I learnt to hold and handle the reins and the stirrups, I became more accustomed to Pavo and able to have thoughts other than ones of falling off her. I could enjoy the views down to the cozily pastoral valley we were leaving. I could look back with nostalgia to scenes from the *Catalina*: the tropical sunsets, Diomidio's fantasies, our first sighting of the Andes. I could feel a sense of achievement on being so close to completing a journey some people thought would be impossible.

For a while I felt as if I were shedding my years, as if I were far nearer to the beginning of my life than to its end, as if I were a boy being taken by his father on some great adventure. But then, just as the climb was developing its own soothing momentum, everything began to change.

Torito abruptly dismounted from his horse, telling us to remain where we were. He wouldn't be long, he said, before dashing up a slope to an isolated wooden shack, the last of the valley's outlying buildings. I stayed mounted on Pavo, trying with diminishing success to prevent her from straying off in search of grass. I hoped Torito would be back soon, but he was mysteriously taking his time.

I tried occupying my mind by studying more carefully the valley we had just climbed. But the panorama's cheerful innocence came to seem as deceptive as that of Quinchana. It was a landscape of ghosts and tragic memories, of killings and kidnappings, of farms taken over by the FARC, of children robbed from their homes, of army searches and reprisals, of inhabitants who had learnt to survive by not telling anyone anything.

Torito finally returned, though without saying a word. Silently we resumed our ascent, with my bones beginning to feel their age as they were jolted by a rapidly narrowing track broken up by rocks and holes. A greater concentration was now needed if we were to avoid accidents. At one point we were forced to swerve dangerously close to the edge of the track to avoid a descending logger who was carrying his load of wood in an ox-drawn cart. The man barely smiled at us as he passed, and gave us a look almost of pity.

Sweat, in the form of a creamy white liquid, oozed from the flanks of Pavo, who nonetheless bore with remarkable patience her heavy and clumsy rider. She was, I decided, a fatalistic horse, hardened by life, at peace with death, prepared for anything that came her way. Capricho, in contrast, began to display what I interpreted at first as a healthy sense of danger. As the ever steeper track was reduced to a line of damp stones she showed emotions that echoed by this stage my own. She started neighing unaccountably and refused to budge any further. She even tried turning round until hit and shouted at by Torito. Reluctantly she continued uphill into a jungle of ferns, lianas and cascading streams. Dark clouds were forming once again above us, adding to the mounting tension in the air, fuelling my misgivings.

We seemed at last to be nearing the top of the mountain, from where, I hoped, the remaining ride to the Páramo would be a mostly undemanding one. But a small and solitary break in the trees showed just how optimistic I was. Ahead of us was an impenetrable-looking landscape of jungle-covered crevices and gorges, from which protruded the occasional crags and vertical escarpments. For the next one and a half days, Torito explained, we would have no other choice but continually to ascend and descend.

My mobile, without a signal since leaving San Agustín, made what would be its final faint beep during my trip to the Páramo. My mother's carer had left me a voice message. I had spoken to her only the day before and had been assured that everything was fine in London. She appeared now merely to be repeating this assurance, though the tone of her voice hinted at something left unsaid. The ambivalence of the message unsettled me. I wondered if I had been wrong to go on this trip, whether I was being as irresponsible as I so often was on my travels, cheerfully setting off somewhere without being properly prepared, confident that luck and optimism would help me through, not thinking enough of the consequences should anything happen.

There was just enough of a signal for me to ring the carer back. She said she hadn't wanted to disturb me, but that my mother had had 'another of her fantasies' and had insisted hysterically that I be rung to find out if I was still alive. My mother wasn't even sure if I was her son. She hadn't taken in that I was in Colombia, nor did this country mean anything to her any more. She had regressed to a state of childhood in which she had recently started calling out for help to her own '*mama* and *pappa*'. But maternal love had evidently survived the absence of memory, and was still so strong that its powers now appeared to defy reason and science, to have given her second sight, to have made her capable of seeing exactly where I was, heading along a precarious track towards somewhere perhaps I should not have been going. She had woken up that morning in a terrible panic, repeatedly shouting out my name, saying that I was in a strange and dangerous land and was about to be killed.

Occasional rustles from the dense undergrowth and the unfamiliar sounds of birds kept me pensive as we penetrated ever deeper into the jungle. Then the path began heading down towards the Magdalena. Going downhill had been my worst memory from previous rides, but I had never known a descent like this, wet, rocky and dizzyingly steep. Pavo lost her footing at least twice and had me holding on tightly to her neck. Torito tetchily noted that I was doing exactly what I shouldn't be doing, and that I should instead be helping the horse by stretching myself backwards. However, the angle of the slope eventually became so impossible that Torito suggested we all dismount and continue on foot.

We finally reached the bottom, where we gladly rested and ate some food next to another of the area's covered bridges. Torito claimed we were almost halfway to the remote farm that would be our base for the next two nights. But when he pointed out the route ahead, I seriously doubted whether Pavo and I would make it much further. On the other side of the river, the sharply ascending path appeared to cling to a section of exposed cliff forming the only break in a sheer slope of jungle.

My legs and lower back were now so stiff that it took me ages to get back onto my horse. Torito, who eventually had to push me, promised that the stretch of path immediately ahead would be the last difficult one of the day. I had learnt not to trust him, though I found it hard to imagine anything as arduous or chilling as the climb we had just started. The path was not really a path at all but rather a steep row of boulders and watery hollows, along which a single slip would probably have been enough to throw Pavo and me into the void.

I tried to keep my eyes looking straight ahead as we neared the cliff I had seen from below. I feared we would find a narrow ledge suspended over a drop of several hundred metres. But we found something else: a rock shelter painted all over with red graffiti.

A chilling memory came back to me as I read the inscriptions, of a trip I had made to Kentucky's lawless borderland with Tennessee. I had been hoping for some relaxing days of hiking with a friend, but what I had got instead was my first introduction to a virgin nature tainted by human menace – crazed hillbillies, gun-slinging pot-growers, a warning sign in dripping red paint, 'Welcome to Varmit County'.

Seeing the name 'FARC', scrawled too as if in blood, made me similarly recoil. All the tales I had read about their atrocities had begun to seem more real to me after hearing first-hand the experiences of ordinary Colombians such as José. I had also seen too many Hollywood films, with their scenes of trigger-happy Latino guerrillas emerging out of the jungle to kill and kidnap passing gringos.

Torito, observing my reaction to the graffiti, dismissed my suggestion that the paint had been recently applied. 'Oh that's been there for years,' he said, pulling on the reins of his horse and hurrying us along. We continued climbing, until eventually the path came out onto a tapering ridge so thick with plants and trees that it took me a few minutes to become aware of the vertigo-inducing drops on either side. Capricho came to an obstinate standstill, and then again three hundred metres further on, after which she became so hysterical that she even managed to resist Torito's fury and head back a few metres towards home. I was now convinced that she was alerting us to something.

But the first drops of rain diverted my thoughts, and obliged us to stop and put on the large capes that Torito had provided us with. Though the downpour did not threaten to last, the discomfort of riding damp along a sodden path with my glasses steaming up was sufficient to numb my initial response to what I thought was a soldier appearing like magic out of the undergrowth. My first thought was that this was one of the Army controls that are still such a feature of travelling in Colombia. Then I noticed the tell-tale rubber boots and the letters FARC on his epaulettes.

He addressed Torito at first before directing his attention at me. After so much nervous anticipation about a situation such as this, I felt curiously calm, partly because I had not yet properly registered the danger I was in, and partly because of the courtesy and friendliness of the man who had stopped us. I had yet to read the autobiography of the politician Ingrid Betancourt, the FARC's most famous recent kidnap victim. She too had been treated with considerable politeness, at the start of what would turn into six years of horrific captivity.

The man who had stopped us announced that he was a member of the Fuerzas Armadas Revolucionarias de Colombia, and asked if I had heard of them. When I said that the name was familiar he told me not to believe the terrible things that were said about them in the press. He then put to me a question to which we would be subjected many more times over the next days. 'Are you frightened of us?' Not at all, I said, beginning at last to become so.

He spoke for a few minutes on a walkie-talkie, then said that 'colleagues' of his were anxious to talk to us about half an hour further up the path. We shook hands with him and went our way, rapt in an anxious silence. To make conversation I asked Torito when he expected us to arrive at our night-time's stop. He estimated that we could get there in about a couple of hours, depending on how long 'they' wanted to speak to us. He told me there was nothing to worry about, that this was going to be just a 'courtesy call' and that everything was going to be absolutely fine. The words 'Tranquilo, no pasa nada' would become an irritating catchphrase of his, said mainly for his own benefit than for ours. He was clearly paralysed with fear.

Julio, characteristically, revealed almost nothing of what he himself was feeling. However, speaking to me for the first time in English, he told me in a whisper not to mention that I was a writer and not to say anything about the book I was planning on the Magdalena. 'Your mother was right,' I said to him. 'Mothers are always right,' he answered with an enigmatic smile.

The rain stopped, and the clouds parted to reveal within the jungle an idyllic small valley partly taken over by pastureland. The guerrillas had occupied what was apparently the penultimate farm before reaching the Páramo. A group of them, mainly smiling young women, was sitting waiting for us under a long wooden portico. I was aware of a couple of them laughing as I clumsily dismounted from my horse.

'Are you frightened?' asked the oldest of the six or so women seated at a table under the portico. She looked in her early thirties, about ten years older than her companions. She had a shock of curly auburn hair, large eyes and a disconcerting, Medusa-like stare. I said as before that I was not frightened at all and that the slight tremble in my hands was due to the cold air and to my being unaccustomed to riding a horse. When I added that I had a sore bum from so many hours in the saddle everyone laughed.

One of the women, together with a grinning boy, got up from their chairs so that Julio, Torito and I could sit down at the table with Medusa. We were brought mugs of coffee, followed by our second lunch of the day – plates full of rice, plantains and offal. It seemed ungrateful and perhaps unwise to say that we had just eaten and in any case had not the slightest appetite.

Medusa was apparently not interested in where we were

from, or what we did, but just wanted to know what opinion we had of the FARC. Did we think of them as the monsters they were usually portrayed as by the press? I said that at my age you didn't take too seriously what was said in the papers. Journalists, like most writers, were invariably liars.

Torito did the rest of the talking. He talked almost without a break, saying that we were tourists who had heard so many wonderful reports about the Magdalena's source, that we were not wealthy tourists, but had hired our horses from humble Quinchana and not from San Agustín, that we were helping the area by sleeping and eating at the farm up the road, and that I was a foreigner with a passionate love for Colombia and its people. Medusa paid no attention to him whatsoever, but instead remained staring at Julio and me, as did a couple of men who had just turned up on horseback. The two men – a muscular Afro-Caribbean and a balding red-haired mulatto – didn't take their eyes off us for a moment as they removed their machetes and machine guns.

When we had managed to eat the last of the food, I tried envisaging some ideal scenario whereby we would thank them for the wonderful hospitality and conversation, and leave. But we were kept waiting around without knowing what we were waiting for. 'Are you frightened?' repeated Medusa, taking us for some reason into the kitchen, after almost an hour more of awkward exchange. We noticed about thirty more guerrillas at the back of the farm, together with a full arsenal of weapons, including rockets and hand grenades.

We also passed a thickset, mustachioed man with a poncho. He gave us a nod by way of a greeting and moved on. He was the only person around in civilian dress. He was the only middle-aged person on the farm. He had a charisma that inspired respect. He must have been the battalion's commander. The FARC commanders were notorious for never wanting to show themselves in public. Now that Julio and I had seen him we would surely never be allowed to go.

In the kitchen we were surrounded by friendly young women, one of whom offered us a pudding she called a *gelatina*. I thought I would be sick if I ate anything else. She tried tempting me by saying that she had made it herself by combining sugar cane with a jelly made from bull's penis. She wrapped it up for me in paper so that I could take it away and eat it when I next felt hungry. She was so kind and sweet and brimming with enthusiasm that I remember thinking what a lovely daughter she would make. Julio asked her how long she had been with the FARC. Since the age of five, she said.

We discovered at last why we were being held. We were waiting for the Deputy Commander, who finally arrived panting, after walking hurriedly across a field. He was wearing a sleeveless camouflage jacket that exposed hairy shoulders. But his Tarzan-like aspect was contradicted by a finely featured head and a kindly, sensitive manner. After apologizing for being late, he launched into a speech.

He said that Colombia was a country of enormous social inequalities. Julio and I were in complete agreement. He then gave us a Marxist discourse of a kind that brought back memories of the 1960s and Seventies. I remembered my days as a devotee of Agit-Prop Theatre and post-revolutionary Cuba, and of the occasion when I attended the one and only meeting of the Courtauld Institute of Art Communist Society. I was almost touched that such idealism had survived unblemished in the Colombian jungle.

We had been standing listening to him for a good half-hour, and the sun was now directly on us. He hadn't asked us anything about ourselves, and in any case was directing his comments entirely to me, the foreigner. He wondered if I had heard of a man called Lenin, but showed only a polite curiosity when I revealed that I had seen the man's embalmed corpse in Moscow. He was determined to convert me to his way of thinking, assuming that Marxism was an ideology that was completely new to me. I found this both endearing and sad, while remaining deeply afraid all the time of where this might lead.

He then gave us the reason why we had been stopped. He said that the FARC was anxious to change the unfairly negative image which people had of the organization. He emphasized how important it was that foreigners such as myself go back to their countries and tell everyone how well the FARC had treated them, and how the FARC was now intending to be a leading promoter of tourism in Colombia.

To the fear that had been mounting in me over the past hours was now added a feeling of experiencing an absurd dream. I had strolled into the pages of *One Hundred Years of Solitude*, witnessing a war that no longer made any sense, a war based on rapidly diminishing memories of how it had started, a war that was kept going almost mechanically, mindless of its shifting, ever more confused objectives.

'The Colombian government', continued the Deputy Commander, 'has done nothing to improve tourism in this province. But when we come to power we're going to do everything possible to change all this. Take, for instance, the path you've been riding on. It's extremely dangerous in its present state. Your horses could have slipped at any moment. We're determined to make a proper wide path with easy grading and good signposting. We also want to build a Visitor's Centre next to the Magdalena's source.'

He looked at his watch and said how sorry he was that he had detained us so long. We were apparently now free to go. Shaking hands with him, and then with all the other guerrillas in turn, we wished them the best of luck with their plans. The girl who had made the *gelatina* said it was a great pleasure to have met me and hoped that we would have a chance to see each other again soon.

As we remounted our horses, waved off by a farewell party of guerrillas, I was half-expecting a bullet in my neck. I only started relaxing after the farm had been left a long way behind. Torito, too, was now breathing normally. He said that in all his years of guiding tourists to the Páramo he had never known anything like this before. He told us not to tell anyone about what had happened. It was as if he were initiating us into his world of secrets and silence.

15

By the end of the afternoon we had reached the farm where we were going to stay. It was the last farm in the valley, the last outpost of civilization before the path climbed up through jungle towards the uninhabited Páramo. It looked the perfect place in which to recover our shattered nerves. Standing in a clearing above the Magdalena, it was a long and simple wooden building, with a big fire-lit kitchen where the warm-hearted mother of the house, Mary, was drying some clothes. A couple of cows were grazing in the fields below, while, further down, Mary's husband Cristian was standing fishing against a backcloth of exotic trees with a purple bloom.

Julio, Torito and I sat out of earshot of him, huddled together on one of the river's boulders. We were going over the events of the afternoon, taking care not to refer to the guerrillas other than as 'our luncheon friends'. Torito now revealed that some of the villagers at Quinchana had warned him of recent 'activity' near the Páramo, but he hadn't taken this seriously. 'There are always rumours. There's normally no truth to them.'

He admitted that he had been very scared, particularly for me, the gringo, whom he hated to think of going away from Colombia with a bad, stereotypical view of his country. 'If, of course, you had gone away at all,' he added, realizing only afterwards that this might not have been the most tactful comment under the circumstances. He began retracting what he had said. 'But they were very good people, very good people. They wouldn't have done anything to you.'

'It was fortunate', joined in Julio, 'that they decided to have a change of policy over the last few days.' I could tell by his amused look that he was thinking exactly the same as I was. As a response perhaps to the pent-up tensions of the past few hours, the two of us burst into a fit of giggles at the thought of the FARC's new contribution to tourism and their projected visitor's centre. I suggested that encounters with our luncheon friends could be included among the list of activities offered by the Hostal La Chaquira.

But this witty banter could not rid me of a growing worry: on our return to Quinchana, the day after tomorrow, we would have to pass the guerrilla encampment again, by which time they might have found out about the friendly relationship I had always enjoyed with the Colombian authorities, or about my visit with ex-president Uribe to the Sierra Nevada de Santa Marta. Or they might have decided already to abandon their unsustainable new image.

'*Tranquilo, no pasa nada*,' said Torito, who repeatedly stressed that today's meeting with the guerrillas was just exceptional bad luck which would never happen again. 'They never stay still in any one place, they're always moving on.' Julio agreed with him, at least for the purposes of reassuring both himself and me. He said that in any case we had no choice now but to continue towards the Páramo. 'I admit I was tempted at one moment to turn back. But that really would have raised suspicions.'

Cristian appeared holding some fish he had caught for our supper. Later, while Mary was cooking them, and the clearly devastated Torito had gone to bed, he came to talk to Julio and me as we paced in the dusk in front of the farm. He hinted that they knew about our unexpected encounter, even though they made no specific mention of the FARC. Two young German tourists, who had stayed with them last night on their way to the colonial town of Popayán, had also met up with 'your friends'. Cristian and his family were obviously concerned that their guests should be having such disturbing experiences. They wanted to put our minds at rest. 'Your friends', Cristian declared, 'are very good people. They are helping Colombia.'

'What else could he say?' shrugged Julio two hours later, as we sat alone in total darkness, biding our time before retiring to our cold and primitive dormitory. 'He and Mary are the ones I feel sorry for. They really are good people. Our luncheon friends say they are fighting for the likes of them, for the *campesinos*. They believe that this gives them the right to take over their homes, help themselves to anything they can find there, and destroy their livelihoods. And after they've gone, along come the paramilitaries or the Army to accuse Cristian and Mary of being collaborators.'

I argued that the guerrillas we had met appeared decent people, driven by a misplaced but genuine idealism. I was saddened by the idea that nearly all of them would die young in the jungle, either through untreated illnesses or killed by the Army. But Julio said that his sympathies were only for those who had become guerrillas without any choice in the matter, 'those poor children robbed from their families at the age of five, and then brainwashed'. However justified the guerrillas were in fighting social inequality, he insisted, 'no human being has the right to rob children, or to inspire such fear in others'.

We ended up talking about fear. The way in which the guerrillas had asked us so many times if we were frightened was something that had made a deep impression on both of us. 'They spend so much of their time being frightened themselves', suggested Julio, 'that they come perhaps to enjoy their power to inspire fear in others.'

The fear I had largely held at bay throughout the afternoon and evening erupted in the course of a near-sleepless night. I worried about having to meet the guerrillas again on our return to San Agustín, about the consequences of our having seen the commander, about the fact that our present whereabouts was known to them. In the absolute silence and darkness of the night every little sound, every barking of a dog, could mean that we were about to have an unwanted visit.

And this thought reminded me of the robber of memories, of the bogeyman, of the legendary person, whoever he was, who turned up on horseback in the dead of night, when least expected. Which in turn set me thinking about my own fear of losing my memory, and about how every time I couldn't remember a word or a name or a face I began to fear that the robber had already come.

And then I realized that my heart was beating uncontrollably fast, and how frightened I was of dying in the middle of the jungle, or being chained here to a tree for so many years that I would join the multitude of the missing and the forgotten.

And then I tried to get a grip on myself. I started remembering my Uncle Brendan, who had helped me so much when I had suffered from panic attacks as an adolescent, who had never lost his faith in reason and humanity, and who had died quoting the poet Dylan Thomas. 'Rage, rage against the dying of the light ...'

I must have slept for a few moments, because Julio, also awake for much of the night, heard me emerging with a scream from a nightmare. I had had one of my recurring dreams about my father. A dream that was not so much a dream but an inerasable memory. A memory of my mother ringing me to tell me to come over as quickly as I could. She said that my father was not expected to last the day. I rushed across London and got there just in time. To hear the rattle.

His eyes, with their vacant stare, were still open when his heart stopped beating. I kissed him on his forehead. I held on to my mother. When I got home the next day I opened the letter he had handed over to me at his club. I was hoping for some revelation that would lessen the sense of chilling finality

I had felt on that rainy, windy day in North Finchley. But the letter, with its business-like tone, was taken up almost entirely with the whereabouts of documents I would need after his death. Only in its last line was there a personal message. He thanked me for all the pleasure I had given him over the years.

We got off to another early start. The Magdalena's source was supposedly five hours' ride from our farm, and we wanted to get back here by nightfall. But after travelling for an hour and a half through a relatively flat stretch of jungle, Torito said that the source was still five hours away. He was more unreliable than he had been the day before, and certainly more distracted. On reaching another covered bridge, just before the climb proper began, he proposed tying up the horses, and taking us on a short uphill detour to see a famous view of a waterfall. For about twenty minutes we climbed behind him through the thick undergrowth until we realized that he was quite lost. I was in a nervous, restless state that morning and did not want to waste any more time. I made Torito turn around.

On our way back to the horses, Julio and I stumbled on an improvised structure made from branches and leaves. This was typical of the jungle dwellings of the guerrillas. We concluded that our luncheon friends were probably scattered everywhere, and secretly observing us. This made me more anxious than ever to move on.

The rocky path, up a dramatic cleft choked by a multi-coloured abundance of strange plants and flowers, was almost impossibly steep, and turned at times into a cascade from all the streams that ran into it. A patch of blue sky hung over the distant summit, which, after a couple of hours of sheer ascent, I began to imagine in terms of Conan Doyle's Lost World.

Further up, the noise of advancing horses diverted me from the difficulties of the climb. Yet the noises were only those of another guide, returning alone with his horses after having accompanied the two Germans whom Cristian had mentioned. He asked Torito in a low voice if we too had encountered the 'purgative'. Then, with a sad and resigned expression, he went his way, leaving us to our final efforts to reach the top.

And then at last we were there, in an exposed moorland landscape of bogs, boulders and bare peaks. This was the Páramo de Las Papas, the earthiness of whose name ('Moorland of the Potatoes') was wholly inappropriate to the otherworldly scenery dotted with the tall, science-fiction-like plants known as *frailejones*. The sun emerged to reward us, and stayed with us after we had reached the point where we had to leave our horses and continue on foot. Torito said how lucky we were. He had been countless times to the Páramo and seen nothing but fog and heavy rain, which had made the Magdalena's source completely inaccessible.

For once I could believe him. Mud and water came over our boots as we persevered in awkward but determined fashion across the marshland. 'To cross the páramo' was an Andean expression meaning 'to die'. But, with the sun above us, and our final destination so near at hand, there was now a death-defying joyousness to my mood, and I remembered the song I had heard in the Barranquilla Carnival Club, about the birth of cumbia in the river that was born in the Páramo de Las Papas, '*Donde nace el Magdalena ... Donde nace la cumbia!*

'DONDE NACE LA CUMBIA!' I wanted to shout as we finally saw the pool that was the Magdalena's source, a translucent swirl speckled with green, a silvery offering in the middle of an eerily monochromatic world. We hurried down to its reedy banks to do what pilgrims supposedly do on attaining this near-mystical goal: we drank from its waters and bathed our faces.

And in the catharsis induced by these two simple acts, I remembered the choice awaiting travellers on arriving at the Underworld: to drink from the spring of Mnemosyne or from that of Lethe. And those who chose the former were awarded an eternity of peace and comfort, while those who wanted to forget – so as to be free of all memories of pains and terrors – were sent back to earth, so that they could learn again the lessons that sufferings bring.

We remounted our horses and prepared for our descent. Having reached the source, I no longer felt as restless as before. And nor did Julio, who began to drag ever further behind, as he stopped to take photos and study flowers. But as Julio and I calmly walked our horses down the watery slope, enjoying the sunlight as it lit up the exuberant flora in the cleft, Torito began urging us to hurry up and stick more closely together. He had been almost jovial in the Páramo, but now he had become jittery and irritable.

I don't know if it was the imminence of the storm he had sensed, or the presence of people around us, but he ordered us to get back on our horses, despite the very real dangers of descending at such a sharp angle, and on such a rocky and wet surface. When Julio ignored him at first, his face contorted with rage.

But he was right about the storm. The almost cloudless sky went rapidly black and the rain started pouring with a force you only find in the tropics. We miraculously succeeded in riding without incident all the way down to the covered bridge, where we waited for a good hour for the rain to stop. Torito declared that he had known rain like this to continue without a break for days on end.

Julio, irritated by Torito, and wishing to spend some quiet moments on his own, decided when we were near the farm to get down from his horse and walk the remaining two kilometres in the dusk. I stayed with Torito, anxious to dry my clothes by the fire in the kitchen.

We found more horses tethered by the farm's entrance. Cristian and Mary's two sons had come from Quinchana, bringing with them the prospect of pleasant company for the night, or at least a welcome alternative to Torito. Two other foreigners were also expected, but, as it was very late, Mary thought they might have had a change of plan.

An hour later, and with still no sign of Julio, there were sounds of new arrivals outside. Two blonde teenage girls entered the kitchen as I was drying my socks by the fire. They were ashen-faced and trembling, and almost tearfully pleased to find someone who could speak English. They were Danes, just arrived in South America, who were taking a six-month break before training to become physical education instructors. They, too, had been detained by the guerrillas, but had been kept much longer than we had. They had been made to dance.

Their guide, a swanky man in a Stetson hat, came into the room, making light of their experiences. He said what good dancers the Danes had been, and that he had taken photographs of them with their 'new friends'. While a lecherous Torito tried to chat up the two girls, the guide took me aside to speak admiringly of the 'friends', and of the good they were doing in the poorer parts of the country. His views seemed brazenly opportunistic. There was also something troubling about his confident manner. I wondered if he was the grave-robber whom Felipe had spoken of.

I was relieved when Julio returned, though he too had news to report. He told me in a whisper that a guerrilla called Marlon had surprised him when he was having a smoke in the forest. Marlon had cadged a cigarette off him, and the two of them had had a long talk. Julio had found out that the guerrillas were likely to be based at the neighbouring farm for a few more days. They had brazenly called for a meeting there with the town authorities of San Agustín. Julio had felt sufficiently emboldened to ask Marlon if it was true that President Chávez of Venezuela was helping to fund the FARC. Marlon said that he didn't know, but then said something that made Julio change the subject immediately. 'There are some people', observed Marlon, 'who ask questions because they are genuinely interested in what we are doing. But there are others who are two-faced and ask because they are spies.'

A hearty supper of fish stew was ready for us. The traumatized Danes were health-conscious vegetarians who wanted nothing more than to go to bed, even though this meant sharing a room with their guide, who had told me with a leer that he had placed his own bed between theirs. Torito and his colleague made every effort to keep them at the kitchen table, while Julio and I, feeling sorry for them, tried to keep up their spirits as the conversation rambled on into another black night.

Just as everyone was ready for sleep the dogs began to bark wildly in the dark. 'They've been disturbed by an animal,' I told the frightened Danes, repeating what Cristian had just said to me. 'It looks as if we might have guests,' corrected their guide.

Marlon and a posse of ten teenage guerrillas walked into the candle-lit kitchen after making the courteous gesture of removing their weaponry. I introduced myself as Julio's friend Michael, while Mary immediately brought out some bowls of the largely uneaten stew. Marlon, a bearded thirty-year-old, in the same sleeveless macho gear as yesterday's Deputy Commander, said that he had heard the Danes were excellent dancers. The women who were with him giggled. Then he shone the torch on me and asked one of them what she thought of me, and whether I would make a good dancing companion. I was a bit too bald for her tastes, she concluded. Everyone laughed again.

I confessed to being a useless but enthusiastic dancer, and that I hoped to improve slightly by the end of my stay in Colombia, when I intended going to the Carnival at Barranquilla. The laughter continued, with all the guerrilla women looking periodically at Marlon as if to have his approval for the light-hearted tone at the table.

The suddenness with which this tone changed was deeply disturbing. Marlon, shifting his position on the chair, and with no trace of a smile remaining, looked directly at me. I began to go clammy. 'Michael,' he said in a slow, ominous voice, 'we have a problem, a very serious problem.'

The darkness half-obscured my trembling hands, which I hoped would not be noticed by the Danes, who were staring at me, anxiously expecting a translation. I wanted them to remain calm, even as I waited in a panic for the news that we were about to be killed or kidnapped. The frustrated father in me was coming to the fore, inducing a surge of protectiveness, and a desire to do something useful and altruistic with what were possibly my final moments. I would plead with Marlon. I would tell him to take me but to spare the Danes and Julio. I loved life, but I had had a relatively full one, while they, on the other hand, had so much happiness in front of them.

Everyone stared at Marlon, wondering what he was going to say. He surprised me once again. 'Michael,' he said, 'the great problem we have in Colombia is that 90 per cent of the land is owned by 1 per cent of the population.' The relief I felt on hearing this gave me the patience for another long Marxist discourse, during which even the other guerrillas started getting bored and walked away. Marlon was determined to exhibit his intellectual credentials, but his speech was a confusing mixture of badly ingested theory and dubious personal views. One moment he was repeating the new FARC policy of encouraging tourism and the next he was saying that tourists who took photos of Colombia without paying were robbers.

Three laughing guerrillas burst into the room with Cristian

in tow, whom they had dressed up in one of their bullet-carrying waistcoats. Cristian seemed to find this as funny as they did, or else he was just pretending to do so, to keep our friends happy. Marlon carried on talking regardless. He was enjoying having new people to impress. His companions, too, were in need of a break from the monotony of jungle life. Visiting the farm was their equivalent of a night out on the town. There was probably nothing more sinister in their motives for being here.

Nonetheless the mixture of guns, extreme youth and Marlon's unpredictable views was one that needed perhaps only the factor of alcohol to ignite. I longed for them to leave, but they were in no hurry. The Danes finally went off to their room, after which their guide, crying almost with laughter, came back to report that they had barricaded the door with a bed. He had had to force himself in.

Marlon stood up at last just before midnight, saying he had a 'busy day tomorrow'. We had no idea where he went after he left. We ourselves were now desperate for sleep, but entered our room to find a pile of machine guns on my bed and an embracing guerrilla couple on Julio's. Torito was hidden under a blanket pretending to be asleep but peeping at the couple.

We returned to the kitchen, where a heavily armed teenage boy from the Colombian Amazonia had now been put on night duty. He had a large head and mad eyes, and spoke with a grin about his hatred of gringos. I assumed that this was his idea of a joke. What really concerned me was the proof that the guerrillas were going to be spending the night with us.

They kindly vacated our room, but the night would be one

of noises and movements. Neither Julio nor I, nor even Torito, got any sleep. A fear more realistic than any we had had so far kept us awake: the arrival of the Colombian Army. We knew that the Army was close at hand, and we knew from Julio's conversation with Marlon that the guerrillas had emerged from hiding to try and make clear to the local authorities who was truly in control of the area. A showdown was inevitable, and we would surely find ourselves in the midst of this, caught up in the crossfire.

The guerrillas had gone by the time we got up. It was a clear dawn and we wanted to get back to Quinchana as soon as possible, hoping for no more relaxing meals with our 'friends'. The Danes, originally on their way to Popayán, had decided to return with us to San Agustín, partly feeling safer in a group and partly because they realized only now that they hadn't enough money to pay their guide and there wasn't a cash point in the village where he was going to leave them. Their naivety matched the innocence of the younger guerrillas.

With our hearts in our stomachs we started off on our return journey. The lush, sparkling beauty of the valley on a fresh, sunny morning briefly distracted me from the fear of soon having to pass the farm of our first day's encounter. But my classical education reminded me of the shepherds who discover in the middle of their bucolic world the tomb which tells them that death, too, stalks Arcadia.

As we nervously climbed a ferny-shaded path towards the farm, we saw a horse and rider descend towards us. Closer by I recognized the young woman who had given me the *gelatina*, her happy, smiling features illuminated by the dappled sunlight. She said she'd known we would meet again. I congratulated her on her pudding, which I had eaten by the Magdalena's source and found delicious. She told me that she was enjoying an early morning outing, and hoped we too were having a good time. And then Torito intervened to tell her that we had a bus to catch at Quinchana, and couldn't stop any longer.

The farm was empty but, long after passing it, Torito kept looking back to make sure no one was watching us. Then the sounds of gunfire broke the Arcadian peace. A young woman guerrilla, Marlon's girlfriend Jenny, was blocking our path and waving us down. The Deputy Commander wanted to talk to me, and he would be with us soon. He and a few others were having some morning gun practice.

When he finally arrived, apologizing as before, he asked me straight away if I knew any English. Usually, he explained, each battalion had its English speaker, but they didn't have one at the moment and urgently needed someone to translate a couple of pages of text. I said I would be delighted to help, if I could, but that my English was rusty through lack of practice. They had clearly mistaken me for a Spaniard.

We rode up to another farm, where Jenny offered us another meal. I said that Spaniards found it difficult to eat much at this time of the morning. While waiting for the text to be brought to me she asked about Spain, about what the Spaniards ate, and about whether the country was also extensively covered in jungle. She had been a guerrilla for most of her life. She had never known what even a large village was like.

The text was an Arizonian manual about how to assemble a laser sight for rifles. My American English, I said, was poor, and my English technical vocabulary almost non-existent. Jenny put her own rifle on the table and started telling me the names of all its parts. Julio, knowing how bad my handwriting was, proposed being my scribe.

Our task was a difficult one, but I took great pride at first in finding exactly the right and most elegant words with which to render the clumsy and barely comprehensible English. But Jenny, like a child who had just been given a toy, was too impatient to wait until I had properly understood the manual. She attempted ham-fistedly to mount the laser sight while repeatedly dropping its tiny screws on the ground. Julio and I were finally obliged to tell her off. 'If you lose those', we told her firmly, as if talking to a daughter, 'this whole thing will be useless.'

I was still playing the consummate professional when Marlon arrived, sweating from the exertions of shooting. He made me nervous as he studied carefully what we were doing. 'Personally,' he reflected after a while, 'I prefer killing somebody at ten metres. But the beauty of this object is that it enables you to do so at a hundred and fifty metres. And in the dark.'

My translation began to lose its meticulousness. I rushed to finish it as quickly as possible, with no concern for how garbled it was. Julio was making the text more useless still by wrongly transcribing some of the phrases I was dictating to him. He was redeeming the two of us for collaborating with the guerrillas.

'The homework's done,' he cheekily announced. We now needed to get away as soon as we could, before another English speaker turned up to declare our efforts intentionally misleading. But still we were detained. Marlon said that the Deputy Commander wanted to speak in private to the two guides, and then to us. '*Tranquilo*,' muttered Torito, '*no pasa nada*.'

Torito and the other guide were gone for about half an hour. They were being instructed to inform all those involved in the tourist business in San Agustín to present themselves at the guerrilla-occupied farm in three days' time. When the FARC summons you, Julio had told me, you have no choice but to obey. Otherwise they'll find you out wherever you are.

We ourselves were merely asked how much we had paid our guides. We lied and said that we didn't know as yet, as everything had been arranged by the person with whom we had been staying in San Agustín. 'The two Germans were charged an exorbitant amount,' commented the Deputy Commander, quoting a figure far smaller than the one Julio and I had agreed to. 'This is very bad for tourism in the area,' he continued. 'If foreigners come here and feel that they are being overcharged, it makes them bitter and unwilling to return. The FARC intends controlling prices to make the area more attractive for tourism.'

I heartedly endorsed this view, and compounded my hypocrisy by eagerly responding to an invitation made by the Deputy Commander after wishing us all a safe journey back. 'The next time you come here, we'll take you to places more beautiful still than the Magdalena's source, places known only to us. Of course you'll have to put up with our simple living conditions, and our homemade tents with their covering of leaves.' Instead of a contact address, he proudly let us know that his particular guerrilla division was the Frente 13 Cacica La Gaitana. He assumed we had heard of them.

A couple more guerrillas stopped us further along the path, to ask once again if we were frightened and what we thought of the new image of the FARC. Though they soon let us go, we remained tense right up to the moment when we came out into the open country looking down towards Quinchana. Only then could we allow ourselves a sigh of relief. We were alive. Elated by this thought, we began our descent into the valley, feeling a momentary sense of pity as we passed a sombre-faced, middle-aged woman riding up into the mountains. 'That was the treasurer from San Agustín's Town Hall,' murmured Torito. 'She must have received her summons.'

We would learn much more over the next two days: that Quinchana was a village controlled by the FARC; that Torito was someone with several children by different women; that he didn't support either his offspring or his exes; that he had been president of the Quinchana village council before committing the ultimate FARC crime of stealing from the village's funds; that the FARC only allowed him back to the area on condition he brought tourists. We would hear, too, the contradictory news that the notorious Frente 13 Cacica La Gaitana had been disbanded, and that the Army was on the point of doing battle with the jungle's remaining guerrillas.

I was happily unaware of all this as I continued riding down into the valley, dreaming of some celebratory drinks and a good night's sleep, and beginning at last to assimilate the intense and swift-changing emotions of the last days – the fear, the anger, the sadness, the amused perception of the utter absurdity of it all. And, as I speculated on how near we had been to death, one thought came to supersede all others. I realized how wrong I had been to dread oblivion, and how consoling instead was the idea of no more thoughts and memories, of having no longer to worry about the future, or to remember anything of the past, with all its mistakes, disappointments and frustrations.

And then I was back in the world of classical mythology. I had travelled to the entrance of the Underworld, where I had drunk from the waters of Forgetting and not from those of Memory. And now I was being punished. By being made to return to earth, to learn all over again.

EPILOGUE

CARNIVAL

On the first morning of Barranquilla's Carnival, on my way to the opening parade, I thought how much I had always wanted to be an actor. I remembered the regular Friday outings to the theatre with my parents and how happy I had been on those occasions, waiting excitedly for the play to begin, seeing my father as I so rarely saw him, relaxed and laughing, with a beam in his deep-blue eyes.

The thrill of those moments was with me now as I arrived by taxi at a broad square dripping with streamers. The city was gradually waking up to the sounds of distant cumbia bands, and the sight of passers-by in masks and wigs. I was with Owen Jones, dredger of the Magdalena, and his glamorous actor wife Rita. He was dressed as a Twenties pimp, with gold in his teeth, and a bright-purple jacket and hat. She was his high-class whore, swirling a cigarette in a silver holder. I was a Chinese mandarin.

Our motley, anarchically costumed carnival group, Disfrázate como Quieras, was slowly gathering along the pavement – clusters of men and women in multicoloured tribal gear, a couple of caimans, a sailor with a funny nose, a Frida Kahlo self-portrait, a giant iPhone, a man with his face in a beer barrel, a mermaid with an inflatable duck, a triton-bearing Neptune, a woman wearing nothing more than a towel and a shower cap. Everyone was chattering away, cracking jokes, commenting on each other's costumes, awaiting orders from the red-bearded master of ceremonies, Gustavo, a museum director disguised as the military leader of some banana republic.

The order finally came to board the bus that would take us as near as it could to the starting point of today's parade. And, in that very moment, I heard the sound that had become for me a harbinger of doom. My mobile was ringing. I tried in a panic to find an opening in my Chinese silks from which to extract it. I managed to, just in time. I answered tremblingly, expecting the call I had feared all along, the sort of call that seems always to come when you're least prepared for it, in the middle of the night, at the crack of dawn, or when you're suddenly feeling that life isn't so bad.

But somehow I knew it couldn't be a call about my mother. She couldn't be dead. I had spoken to her yesterday and she had sounded almost normal. Her appetite had returned. She had sung lines from an Italian song. She could probably go on living like this for years, surviving everyone else in the family, condemned to a seeming eternity of forgetting.

'It's Julio,' said the voice at the other end of the line. He appeared agitated. He asked if I was able to speak to him. He apologized for phoning so early, and hoped that the parade had not yet begun. But he had just received a disturbing message from San Agustín.

The message, crackling, truncated and confused, had been left by Felipe at four in the morning. Felipe, desperate to speak to him, had either gone to his meeting with the FARC, or else the FARC had gone to see him at La Chaquira. The unmistakable voices of Marlon and the Deputy Commander could be heard in the background. They were demanding to know the whereabouts of the 'elderly' gringo and his younger Colombian friend. The message was then curtailed by what sounded like shooting.

Julio had gone to a public phone box to try and ring Felipe, but had been unable to contact him. However, he had got hold of Torito, who had repeated rumours of an imminent Army attack. They had arranged to speak again later in the day, by which time Torito might have more news to report. Julio would try in the meantime to find out if there were any real danger of the FARC tracking us down. He thought I was safe in carnival-time Barranquilla, but that I was probably wise to be leaving for Europe the next morning. He said he might have to join me.

Anarchy was breaking out. The bus left us at a place where many other carnival groups began mingling with ours as we streamed down a broad, packed, noisy, treeless avenue in search of our allotted position in a parade not due to begin until several hours later, when the sun would be at its hottest. Owen and Rita, the pimp and his whore, became my main points of reference as I threaded my way through the chaos of costumes, trying not to think too hard about what Julio had just told me, but beginning nonetheless to perceive some of the masked faces around me as fragments of a macabre vision, their jollity dark and sinister, their gestures threatening, their shouts abusive and cautionary. I could not get out of my head the idea that someone in this grotesque crowd was looking for me.

But soon I did. The emotional exorcism that was perhaps the ultimate purpose of the carnival was taking effect even as we approached the colourfully draped truck serving as our group's processional float. Massive speakers, attached to its sides, were booming out all the carnival classics, while Gustavo, raised on a platform in the middle, was standing with microphone in hand inciting us all with an insistent, accelerating chorus of '*Disfrázate como quieras! … Disfrázate como quieras! … Disfrázate como quieras! …*'

His olive-green cap, bobbing up and down above the surging crowd, was like a beacon to which were drawn the group's full complement of members, among whom were people I knew from all over Colombia, people I had never suspected as carnival devotees, people whom I had never imagined meeting again, let alone in Barranquilla. There were exchanges of surprise and joy, a warm hug from Jaime the Devil, a wink from Carlos the Sun God, a slapping of hands with John Lennon, great kisses from a trio of sacrificial virgins, and so many glasses of a cold rum punch that every new encounter became progressively more blurred and hallucinatory, until the dancing took over, passionate, unrestrained, unstoppable.

And so it continued after the parade had finally got going, dancing and drinking with barely a break, between crowded stands, watched by spectators who themselves were swaying to the infectious music, cheering us on, pressing right up to the barrier, sharing our rum, asking to be photographed in the arms of a Chinese mandarin.

The mask, with its tiny slits for eyes, took away what was left of my inhibitions, heightened the unreality of the occasion, and slowly tunnelled my vision, so that in the end, as the sunlight rapidly faded and a drugged state of exhaustion set in, all I seemed to be seeing were hundreds of staring eyes, which I began dizzily to scour, in a crazed, irrational search for those caiman-like eyes I had encountered on that distant occasion in Cartagena, those unforgettable eyes that had inspired my journey, and which were surely somewhere here in Barranquilla, still watching over me, still guarding memories of a magical Magdalena unfolding towards oblivion.

'All over.' I didn't read Julio's cryptic message until after nightfall, as the weary remnants of our group reassembled at the Carnival Club, and mascara was smudged on sweating faces, and raw feelings were coming to the surface, and uncomfortable truths being told. I rang him back from the quietest corner in the garden.

He said he had spoken again to Torito, who confirmed that

the Army had intervened two days after we had left the area. They had bombed the jungle stronghold, and had probably killed all the guerrillas we had known. Cristian and Mary were fine, he assured me, but no one had managed so far to speak with Felipe. He had disappeared.

Sleep was what I now needed most, a deep, undisturbed sleep that would calm the strong emotions that were welling again inside me. But my persuasive friend Jaime Abello, still in his devil's costume, lured me to another party, in another part of the city, saying that I would have all the time in the world to sleep the next day, and that sleeping was in any case an activity best left for when I was home in Europe, for who knows when I would be coming back to Colombia, or whether I would ever have the opportunity to return to the Barranquilla carnival, the best carnival in the world.

So I went with him later that night to a courtyard covered in flowers, masks and fairy lights, full of familiar faces, of waiters plying me with exotic cocktails, of beautiful women telling me that it didn't matter how badly I danced, for what was important was to abandon myself completely to the ever more urgent music, a music that stirred up so many poignant memories and which was now bringing out all the sadness mounting behind my Chinese grin.

The mask shielded my tears when these eventually came, at the end of the last dance, as I sat down breathless and perspiring on a chair. I had a memory of the enthusiastic young guerrilla woman who had hoped to meet me again and was now probably dead. I saw her as vividly as I had seen my father laughing in the theatre. I saw her full of the joy of life, riding towards me on a bright, sunny morning, and then riding away, never to find the parents she barely remembered, never to be remembered herself.

Jaime, who noticed everything, was sitting next to me. 'Michael,' he said, 'your problem is that you think too much.' And then he uttered the two words that still come to me whenever I think of my parents, of my Uncle Brendan, of all those I know whose minds have gone, of all the people who have meant so much to me and whom I shall never see again: '*Carpe diem.*'

FURTHER READING

Abad Faciolince, Hector, *Oblivion: A Memoir*, 2010

Chao, Ramón, *The Train of Ice and Fire: Mano Negra in Colombia*, 2009

Castaño Uribe, Carlos, *Río Grande de la Magdalena, Colombia*, 2003

Celestino Mutis, José, *Viaje a Santa Fe*, 1991

Cochrane, Charles A., *Journal of a Residence and Travels in Colombia During the Years 1823 and 1824*, 1825

Consejo Vargas, Yolanda (ed.), *Sin volver ni haberse ido*, 2008

Davis, Wade, *One River: Explorations and Discoveries in the Amazon Rain Forest*, 1996

Feiling, Tom, *Short Walks from Bogota: Journeys in the New Colombia*, 2012

Franzen, Jonathan, 'My Father's Brain' in *How to Be Alone*, 2002

García Márquez, Gabriel, *One Hundred Years of Solitude*, 1970

García Márquez, Gabriel, *Chronicle of a Death Foretold*, 1982

García Márquez, Gabriel, *Love in the Time of Cholera*, 1988

García Márquez, Gabriel, *The General in his Labyrinth*, 1990

García Márquez, Gabriel, *Living to Tell the Tale*, 2002

Gómez Isa, Felipe (ed.), *Colombia en su laberinto: Una mirada al conflicto*, 2008

Gomez Picon, Rafael, *Magdalena: Río de Colombia*, 1951

Gómez Valderrama, Pedro, *La otra raya del tigre*, 1977

Hemming, John, *The Search for El Dorado*, 1978

Holton, Isaac, *New Granada: Twenty Months in the Andes*, 1857

Isherwood, Christopher, *The Condor and the Cows: A South American Travel Diary*, 1949

Martin, Gerald, *Gabriel García Márquez: A Life*, 2009

Merrill Block, Stefan, *The Story of Forgetting*, 2008

Muñoz, Humberto, *El Magdalena, Mi Vida: Memorias de un Naviero*, 2009

Murillo, Amparo, *Un mundo que se mueve como el río: Historia regional del Magdalena Medio*, 1994

Museo Nacional de Colombia, *Mutis al natural: Ciencia y arte en el nuevo reino de Granada*, 2008

Museo Nacional de Colombia, *Río Magdalena: Navegando por una nación*, 2nd edition, 2010

Nichols, Theodore E., *Tres puertos de Colombia: Estudio sobre el desarrollo de Cartagena, Santa Marta, y Barranquilla*, 1972

Niles, Blair, *Colombia: Land of Miracles*, 1924

Noguera Mendoza, Anibal (ed.), *Crónica grande del río de la Magdalena* (2 vols), 1980

Palacios, Marco, *Legitimacy and Violence: A History of Colombia, 1875–2002*, 2006

Reichel-Dolmatoff, Gerardo, *San Agustín: A Culture of Colombia*, 1972

Shenk, David, *The Forgetting: Understanding Alzheimer's: A Biography of a Disease*, 2001

Simons, Geoff, *Colombia: A Brutal History*, 2004

Smith, Stephen, *Cocaine Train*, 2000

Yates, Frances, *The Art of Memory*, 1966

ACKNOWLEDGEMENTS

I have always enjoyed the most wonderful hospitality, courtesy and friendliness in Colombia, even during the most adverse moments. For sharing so many strange and memorable experiences along the Magdalena with such good humour I am grateful above all to Julio Caycedo, an ideal travelling companion.

Among the many others who have enhanced my Colombian journeys, I would like to give special mention to: Hector Abad Faciolince, Jaime Abello Banffy, Natalia Algarrín Gutierrez, Yimi Alvarado Martínez, Ana María Aponte Escobar, María Paula Bacquero, Gustavo Bell, Rita Bendek, Betuel Bonilla, Teresa Castrillón, Yolanda Consejo Vargas, Juan Esteban Constaín, Juan Daniel Correa, José Cueca, Edward Davey, Francisco De Castro, Constanza Escobar, Luis Fernando Franco, Pedro Franco, Cristina Fuentes, Julio Galvis, Gabriel

García Márquez, Izara García Rodríguez, Pascual Gavira, Angela Gómez, Catalina Gómez, Gloria Isabel Gómez, Oscar Guardiola-Rivera, Adriana Guzmán Staza, Alejandro Henao, Andrés Hoyos, Camilo Jímenez, Owen Jones, Mario Jursich, Dr Francisco Lopera, Siobhan Maguire, Nando Marchena, Ezequiel Martínez, Ibsen Martínez, Alejandro Mendoza, Juan Alberto Montoya, María José Montoya, Daniel Mordzinski, Ricardo Moreno, Liliana Nelson, Rainbow Blue Nelson, Mariela Osorio, Silvia Ospina, María Bernardo Palomino, Victor Peña, Pablo Pérez, María Cristina Pimiento, Marianne Ponsford, Margarita Posada, Milena Ramírez, Mauricio Restrepo Gil, Liliana Reyes, Guido Ripamonti, Obdulio Quinto Robles, Dagoberto Rodríguez Aleman, Izara Rodríguez, Stefany Romero, Renson Said, Owen Sheers, Paula Silva, Betty Sinning, Andrés Felipe Solano, Luis Humberto Soriano, Paula Spá, Miguel Taborada, Thierry Ways, Gaby Wood, Rod Wooden and Johanna Zuleta.

NAVESCO and the Naviera Fluvial de Colombia provided invaluable help, as did the organizers of the Hay Festival at Cartagena, and the ever generous Colombian government organization Proexport. My thanks as well to the inspirational Colombian ambassador in Britain, Mauricio Rodríguez; to the London head of Proexport, Juan Guillermo Pérez; to my discerning agent, David Miller; and to the Baroness Beatrice Monti von Rezzori, in whose Tuscan paradise at Donnini I put the book's finishing touches. I owe an especial debt to the unfailingly supportive staff at Granta Books, in particular my brilliant editor Bella Lacey, who encouraged the direction the book eventually took and whose many suggestions have immeasurably enhanced the text.

Finally, and as always, I must thank Jackie Rae and all those friends and family members who have sustained me during my periods of writing in Britain and Spain. This book is dedicated to the memory of two of my most loyal supporters, my uncle Brendan Jacobs, and Jackie's brother Tom Rae.